SCRAPSTASHTIC QUILTS:

Organizing Your Scrap Fabric Stash and ACTUALLY USING IT

By Janellea Macbeth

Copyright 2015 Janellea Macbeth. All rights reserved.

Except for use in the reviews for this book, the reproduction or utilization of this work in whole or in part, in any form, is strictly prohibited. Printable excerpts of this book are available at www.janelleamacbeth.website/excerpts, and may be used for personal use only. For class, guild, and workshop use, please purchase one copy of the book for each participant, or request (and receive) written permission from the author. The author can be reached at Amored.Flaneur@gmail.com.

Macbeth, Janellea (2015-09-22). ScrapStashtic Quilts: Organizing Your Scrap Fabric Stash and Actually Using It. Kindle Edition.

ISBN-13: 978-1517528614

ISBN-10: 1517528615

My Newsletter, Reviews, and How to Get Free Stuff!

Thank you so much for purchasing this book. Quilting is such an important part of my life, and I really enjoy making new quilting friends. I would love for you to contact me and keep in touch, in one of many ways:

First, please visit my website, www.janelleamacbeth.website/. There, you will find information about books I've written, a picture gallery, and my blog. Most importantly, however, you will also find the opportunity to sign up for my newsletter. This is a spam-free newsletter, and I only email a few times a month. Topics will vary from new ideas that might interest you, the occasional special promotion, and cool stuff I am giving away, such as signed copies of my book or free, top-notch quilting goodies!!!!

Next, I'd really like to get your opinions of the book. I would REALLY appreciate it if you would leave a frank and candid review on Amazon! Reader reviews are the lifeblood of any author's career. For me, as an author, getting reviews (especially on Amazon) means I can submit my book for advertising, which means I can actually sell a few copies from time to time. Every review means a lot to me!

I'd also like to get to know you and keep in touch. You can find me on Facebook at www.facebook.com/amored.flaneur?fref=nf. Don't worry; I don't overuse my Facebook the way many people do. Rather, it serves as a great way to share ideas, videos, and inspiration with other quilters and artistic crafters from all over.

Additionally, I would love to hear about your ideas, opinions, projects you are working on, books you are reading, or any quilt wisdom you would like to share. I especially love to celebrate 'Ah-ha!' moments and finished projects. Quilt pictures are welcome! Feel free to post to my Facebook, or send me an email at amored.flaneur@gmail.com.

Acknowledgements

This book may have started as a figment of my imagination, but it never would have come to life without the significant help of some very special people. In chronological order:

Thank you, Mom, for making sewing a way of life. Thank you, Derek, for getting published first. As much as I pushed you to write, it was your publishing deal that made me wonder what I was waiting for!

Thank you, Kelsey, for having (and using) your computer wizardry to build every. Single. Graphic. In this book.

Thank you, Dave, for rebuilding my Gammill. Again.

Thank you to my beta readers, for catching all of the details that I missed. Any errors that remain are my fault, entirely. Sharon Sakellion, Jen Walker, Becky Petersen, and Kathy Stadler of www.Patchwork-Pro.de, your input on this project was priceless.

Thank you, Kelsey, for learning how to build a website for me. Twice.

Thank you, Tia Kelly, for holding my hand on Facebook.

And, thank you, Kelsey, for being the other half of my brain for the duration of this project. You were doomed to learn how to quilt, one way or another....

In Loving Memory

Yuki, you were a pest, but I wish you could help me sew, one more time.

Table of Contents

Introduction 9
What Is Scrap Quilting, and Why Should You Do It?..................... 12
How to Implement the ScrapStashtic System................................. 15
Standard Sizes 22
How to Organize Your Scraps, and Use Them Continually 27
Quilt Recipes 29
Overall Design Guidelines 51
How to (Mostly) Avoid Making Ugly Quilts 53
Design Troubleshooting... 55
Scrap-Quilt Definitions 56
Nuts And Bolts... 58
Extra Credit... 60
For the truly committed scrap quilter 60
Stay in Touch with the Author 64

Introduction

Why There Are No Photographs in this Book

There are no photographs of quilts in this book. This is INTENTIONAL. The graphics have been painstakingly created to help you understand the quilt construction, design elements, and the versatile permutations that can be rendered from each quilt 'recipe.' By keeping the graphics abstract, I have given you the ability to apply your own creative statement to your ScrapStashtic quilts. I want you to use this book to nurture your quilt design creativity and learn how to design your quilts based on the constraints of the supplies you have on hand.

Once you become comfortable with the design skills you will acquire through using the ScrapStashtic system, you will be able to improvise scrap quilts with ease.

Ultimately, I would love for you to have the quilting confidence to be able to say, 'All I need to design a one-of-a-kind piece of art is my brain, and my fabric.'

About the Author

Hello, and thank you so much for buying my new book! It's always a leap of faith when you follow directions from an author you have never sewn with before, and this book isn't quite like any other quilt book I have ever seen. Let me give a bit of background on my sewing journey, and along the way, I'll give you a peek at how this book and the ScrapStashtic system grew out of my sewing habits.

First of all, my name is Janellea Macbeth, but I only use my full name when I really want to catch your attention. (If you sing my first name to the tune of the Hallelujah Chorus, you should get the pronunciation and the tone inflection right.) My friends all call me Jan, and you are certainly welcome to, as well!

Apparently, I was a fussy baby who never slept. The closest thing to a nap my mom could coax me into trying was to watch her sew. Some of my earliest memories are of watching the blue sparks inside the motor of my mom's Singer. I can't think of a time when I didn't have my own sewing scissors, and I spent my toddler years carving up fabric scraps into no-sew doll clothes.

> Please visit my website, http://www.janelleamacbeth.website. There, you will find information about books I've written, a picture gallery, and my blog. Most importantly, however, you will also find the opportunity to sign up for my newsletter. This is a spam-free newsletter, and I only email a few times a month. Topics will vary from new ideas that might interest you, the occasional special promotion, and cool stuff I am giving away, such as signed copies of my book or free, top-notch quilting goodies!!!!

When I was three, my mom let me use her sewing machine unsupervised. Guess what!?!! I still have all of my fingers, and knock on wood, have never caught a finger in the machine. I progressed very quickly from drawstring bags, aprons, and handkerchiefs to scrunchies, shorts, and dresses.

I had moved on to tailoring wool and linen suits around the age of nine. I also started hand piecing 1930's quilt patterns as a hobby. (I loved the 80's pastel calicos and went to town with 8-point stars, Dresden plates, and grandmother's flower garden.) I was still, however, primarily a garment sewer.

As I entered middle school, suits were not impressive enough to use in competition any longer, and so I switched to sewing high end costumes, similar to the costumes that are used in cosplays today. By the time I was an underclassman in high school, I began making and designing formalwear. At 17, I became a Civil War Re-enactor, and my interests shifted to historically accurate construction. In two years, I made a complete wardrobe, including undergarments and a custom drafted corset.

It was at this point that quilting became more than a passing hobby between sewing competitions. I switched to machine piecing and rotary cutting (unless I was doing piecework at a re-enactment), and all of my quilts were 1860's (or earlier) reproductions. I hand quilted everything, occasionally with a hoop, but mostly with a trestle and rails quilt frame.

By the time I went to college, I didn't have room in my 1860's wardrobe for more pieces. So while at school, I joined a renaissance ensemble with a costume closet that hadn't been updated since the 1960's. Guess who they dubbed costume mistress? Between my junior and senior year in college, I replaced 90% of the costumes that were being used in performances.

And then, there were the dark years...

I had spent the last 20 years sewing for fame and fortune. (Well, mostly for envy and praise, but who's counting?) And, I came to the conclusion that I am not a nice person when I compete. I was tired of being that not-nice-person, and so I walked away from sewing. Cold Turkey. I went from making 30 to 50 high-end, high-skill garments every year to making one or two slapped together outfits: an improvised dress to wear when chaperoning prom. A set of tailored wizard robes for a Harry Potter book release party. My wedding dress. The bridesmaid's dresses. The groomsmen's suits. Ok, the wedding stuff wasn't slapped together. That was a year of sweatshop sewing on every weekend and school holiday. (Being a teacher gave me lovely holidays to dedicate to sewing, but no time to sew in the evenings after work.)

Around that time, I 'threw the baby out with the bathwater,' and more or less stopped quilting as well. Meanwhile, my mom treated her empty nest syndrome with fabric therapy, and plunged head first into the quilting world with gusto. She joined guilds and went to workshops. She bought every book under the sun, and traveled to exotic quilt stores. She went to conventions, and tried every technique ever. And by golly, if she was learning about it, I had to, as well, whether I wanted to or not. (Mostly not at that point in my life, but since my mom wanted me to learn, I did.)

Through my mom, I learned fussy cutting, and paper piecing, one-block-wonder, puzzle balls, bargello, double wedding ring, split 9-patch, needle turn appliqué, quilt-in-a-

Introduction

day, stitch-and-flip, crazy quilting, couching, whole cloth quilting, signature quilts, red work, art quilting, circular piecing, Baltimore album quilts, William Morris repros, hand dyeing, crayoning, stenciling, free motion machine quilting, quilting on a domestic machine, using the Flynn frame, water color quilts.... The list goes on and on. I learned it all, quietly kicking and screaming, but politely storing the wealth of knowledge and skill because it might be useful. Someday. (Yeah, sure, Mom....)

And then one day, when I was a new stay-at-home mom, my own mother dragged me to a quilt show to show off her new grandbaby to all of her friends. I hadn't been in a fabric store in YEARS, and I was amazed by the changes in the quilt fabric industry since I had last tumbled down the rabbit hole.

But what stopped me dead in my tracks, and made me fall off the fabric-free-wagon was a Mini Charm Pack. A cute, harmless little 2½" x 2½" set of 42 different squares... all from the same line of fabric. It found its way into my hand, and I couldn't put it down. The attraction was magnetic, the fabric was compelling. And as I stood there, teetering on the brink of falling back into addiction, I made myself a few promises:

- I would never buy more fabric than I could use in a reasonable amount of time.
- I would keep my tools and supplies to a minimum so that my house didn't disappear under a pile of fabric.
- I would ONLY sew for fun, and would not turn into a crazy perfectionist.
- I would NEVER compete again. (Remember? I'm not nice when I compete.)

I'm sure you can tell that not all of those rules have lasted as I have plunged deeper and deeper into the quilting world, but I do still adhere to the essence of them. I never compete, and I still view neatness as a side effect of skill, rather than an end goal. I sew 2-15 hours a day in the winter, so it must still be fun, and if I tried really hard, I could sew away all of my fabric in six months. Rule number two is where I often fall short, as my collection of rulers and books has grown tremendously, and I do still occasionally binge on buying fabric.

But, for the most part, I am very happy with the way that I sew, the way that I interact with my fabric, and the relationship I have with my stash. It has taken some hard, internal work to figure out how I most enjoy sewing, and this book is a portion of what I do to keep some of the promises listed above. I hope this book helps you find some clarity, give some charity, and enjoy yourself at the sewing machine!

What Is Scrap Quilting, and Why Should You Do It?

What is scrap quilting?

Scrap quilting is technically any project that uses leftover fabric from other projects. Initially, American patchwork was born of the need to reuse every small piece of fabric that could be salvaged from clothing that was too worn to mend further. It was a solution to a desperate situation that evolved into a feminine art form as the American Colonies emerged in the world economy.

Unless you are working on a sentimental quilt, I do not recommend using clothing scraps because most modern clothing contains at least some synthetic fibers, which make it more difficult to keep your quilting neat and even. While I am not a neatness-nancy when it comes to quilting, I do believe that there should be a general neatness that comes with quilting as a byproduct of your inherit skill level. The other reason that I do not endorse scrap quilting from used fabric is the stress on the fabric. Reused fabric will wear more quickly than fresh fabric, and mixing used and new fabric will increase the risk of your quilt shredding in the future.

Fun Fact:

When America was first settled, European ships would drop off colonists for 1-4 years to either survive and thrive, or disappear like the lost colony of Roanoke. They had a few basic supplies from the civilized world, but once their manufactured goods were consumed, they had to make do with what they had. In the early era of American colonization, quilting was a functional skill that kept the colonists from freezing to death. Quilts were stuffed (yes, stuffed, not filled with batting) with straw, leaves, grasses, and moss.

Why should you scrap quilt?

Scrap quilting can be a great frustration to quilters who don't naturally gravitate to scrapping. If you read my book, and scrap quilting STILL doesn't appeal to you, make friends with a scrap quilter (or six) in your guild, share my methods, and pass your scraps on to your new friends in a way that they can use them.

However, if you are looking for motivation to start scrap quilting yourself, here it is:

There are so many intrinsic reasons why scrap quilting is a great habit to cultivate. It is peaceful, easy, repetitive sewing, leaving lots of room for contemplation. It forces you to look at the big picture because you are not necessarily following a planned out color scheme, and big-picture thinking translates well to real life. It inspires unusual color combinations, which can be extrapolated to your primary quilt design, because it is a 'safe' place for wild experimentation. Also, for the same reason, it lets you explore your inner child and celebrate your creativity.

When you are comfortable enough with experimenting with these quilts, you will find that scrap quilts tend to serve as a snapshot of your quilting identity; your style will mutate over the months and years, and your scrap quilts can highlight and honor these subtle changes. Most importantly, your scrap quilts will all be truly one-of-a kind quilts that showcase your personality.

One of my friends described it perfectly, about the scrap quilt I had made for her, and so I asked her to write a short note for this book. This is what she handed to me, word for word:

> *"The quilt Jan made for me is among my most treasured possessions, for one reason. It's not that it's fancy, or because of the work she put into it, or the cost of the fabric, though I am definitely aware of those aspects. I love it because every inch of it shows her personality as a quilter, in what patterns she used in different areas, and which fabrics she put together. I love it because her personality is stamped all over it. To me, personality takes precedence over all other qualities."*
> *– Kelsey O'Connell*

There are extrinsic reasons, too. Scrap quilting is hailed as the 'great money saver.' When you buy quilt fabric, you spend $8-$15 per yard. The scraps that you THROW AWAY also cost $8-$15 a yard, and if you think that you aren't throwing away YARDS of scrap fabric, you probably aren't doing as much quilting as you think you are. (Or you are deceiving yourself to keep your wallet - and your husband - from complaining.)

Scrap quilting also STRETCHES your money, because you are using MORE of the fabric you have already purchased. Scrap quilting saves you money because the time you spend making quilts from your scraps will mean that you are buying new fabric less frequently. You will still make new projects, but because you will whip up a few scrap quilts for the local charity you will be able to spend more time quilting without drastically changing the amount of money you invest in your hobby. More quilting is always an excellent idea, isn't it?

The fear of waste is a huge motivator for many scrap quilters. I mentioned the waste of money above, but it is starting to become popular to give more consideration to the waste of resources and the subsequent strain on our environment. All of those scraps that you have thrown away in past years have an inherent carbon footprint leftover from their manufacturing process, and once you throw them away, they accrue a SECOND environmental debt in the local landfill. By using more of the fabric you already purchase, you are justifying more of the carbon footprint AND you are reducing the volume of trash in the landfill.

When I think of waste related to quilting, I have a slightly different perspective. The biggest factor I consider about waste in quilting is wasted space. Every square foot of fabric that is stored in my house BUT IS NOT BEING USED is wasting my energy and my tax money. I pay taxes on the square footage of my home when I pay property taxes. If the space is filled with quilting fabric, then I am paying money to store things that I have already spent money to purchase, am now paying to heat or cool (based on the season), and am paying an emotional debt on the guilt of UFO's. (Un-Finished Objects.) I am also losing the use of the square footage that is filled with fabric. Ask yourself: would I rather have a beautiful, large stash that sits around for years and years? Or would I rather have a modest stash with room to work and permission to buy new fabric whenever I want to?

Why do I need a system for scrap quilting?

Many people find scrap quilting overwhelming, uninteresting, or complicated. A scrap quilting system will help you overcome some resistance to trying out this type of quilting by simplifying the variables in making a scrap quilt. Without a system, scraps accumulate in forgotten corners of your sewing room and ultimately overrun your space. A scrap system should not only organize your scraps, but also remind you when they need to be used, and make it fun and easy to do so.

If you don't naturally fall into a habit of scrap quilting, you will need a system that will make it easy to do scrap quilts. (Any system; it doesn't have to be mine!) There are some amazing pioneers out there, and the important thing is to find a system that you like enough to stick with in the long run. (It took me about 2 years to develop my system, and have now been using the system successfully for at least three years already.)

What do I mean when I say system?

A system is any process or generic set of actions that will consistently produce the desired results. When it comes to scrap quilting, I use the word 'system' to refer to the process of saving, cutting, storing, and using fabric left over from other completed projects. My system funnels your scraps quilt recipes, which are different than patterns because they provide a framework of design guidelines rather than rigid step-by-step instructions. Traditional instructions limit the creativity and permutations that the quilter can use. Working with scraps gives you the freedom to design your own quilt based on the fabric you have available and using this 'recipe' system means that the design can be altered in many ways with ease. Like a diet or fitness system, my scrap quilting system gives you an overall action plan as well as specific steps to take in order to change your relationship with your leftover fabric from a passive relationship to an active one.

What are the benefits of implementing the ScrapStashtic System?

- Using your scraps means you buy less new fabric, minimizing expenses and simultaneously reducing your carbon footprint.
- Stretch the use of the money you've already spent
- Increase your charity quilt production
- Reduce the amount of fabric that takes up space in the landfill, or completely cease to contribute ANY fabric to the landfill
- Reduce the amount of fabric in your house that you 'Should use, someday…'
- Design one-of-a-kind quilts every time you sew
- Spend more time quilting!

How to Implement the ScrapStashtic System

How long does it take to learn the ScrapStashtic System?

It should only take about 15 minutes to learn the basics of the ScrapStashtic System if you are already invested in learning to scrap quilt. If you want to take the fast route to getting started, you can skip right to the 'Implementation' section. However, to get the full benefit of the system, you should probably read all of the info that I have given you about what the system is, how it works, and why you should try it. Feel free to skip around, but reading this book will give you lots of inspiration to get out there and sew.

The short version

- ->Read the book and look over the quilt recipes to make sure you like the system enough to invest your time in it.
- ->Choose your storage solutions. With the exception of my Jelly Roll container, all of my storage bins are smaller than a standard shoebox.
- ->Choose a scrap bowl for scraps that are waiting to be fussy cut. Your bowl should be about the size of a shallow soup bowl so that you have to empty it frequently. (Trust me, it's not fun to spend 6 hours carving up scraps out of a full sized storage bin. It's much easier to empty a bowl in 20-30 minutes several times a month.)
- ->*Optional:* choose a Schnitzel trashcan that ONLY receives fabric and batting SCRAPS. I use these scraps to stuff toys to donate to the local hospitals for children in need, but you can use them for whatever you'd like. Another idea is to make your own dog toys or pet beds for the local animal shelter. My favorite toy recipes are included with the quilt recipes, and can help you reduce your fabric waste to ZERO.
- ->Choose your 'standard sizes' based on the requirements of your favorite quilt books or patterns. My sizes are 2" squares, 2½" squares, 2 7/8" squares, 1¼" to 3" strips, random lengths, and 2½" x 40" strips. (Also, for flannel fabric only, I prefer 3" squares. See the note about flannel, included in the 'Standard Sizes' section.) These are the sizes that I use for the recipes included in this book. However you could use any sizes that you would prefer so long as they are complementary. Keep in mind that the more scrap sizes you select, the more storage you will need and the longer it will take you to accumulate enough scraps to make a quilt.
- ->Fussy cut your scraps when your scrap bowl is full, and place your pre-cuts in their storage bins.
- ->Carve up your backlog of scraps as you feel inspired to.
- ->When a 'standard size' bin fills up, make a quilt using those precuts.

ScrapStashtic Quilts

The longer explanation

-> Read the book and look over the quilt recipes to make sure you like the system enough to invest your time in it. Reading the whole book will provide you with inspiration to go out and sew. It will also convince you to use your scraps instead of throwing them away or storing them to use 'someday.'

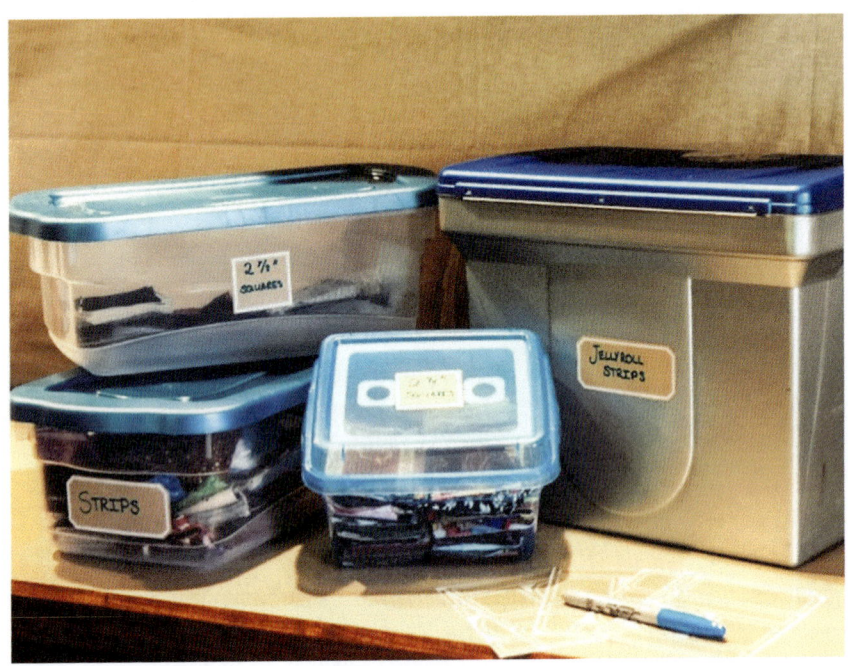

-> Choose your storage solutions. With the exception of my Jelly Roll container, all of my storage bins are smaller than a standard shoebox. Most of my small storage bins come from the dollar store, although one of them is a convenient cardboard box, and another is a pretty box that came with a mug I love. My Jelly Roll bin is a plastic file box. All of your containers should have lids to keep the dust out, and should be large enough to keep your precut squares flat. The 'strip' bins should be empty enough to keep the folded strips from creasing.

-> Choose a scrap bowl for scraps that are waiting to be fussy cut. Your bowl should be about the size of a shallow soup bowl so that you empty it frequently. (Trust me, it's not fun to spend 6 hours carving up scraps out of a full sized storage bin. It's much easier to empty a bowl in 20-30 minutes several times a month.) I recommend a bowl for this portion of the system for several reasons. First of all, you need to keep your waiting scraps in one place so that you can SEE when it's time to fussy cut. The bowl keeps the scraps neat and also serves as a visual cue for WHEN there are enough scraps to carve. I also like a bowl because every time you look at it, you will be reminded that your fabric will wrinkle if you leave it in a curved container for too long, which adds another level of motivation.

How to Implement the ScrapStashtic System

-> *Optional:* choose a Schnitzel trash can that ONLY receives fabric and batting scraps. I then use these scraps to stuff toys to donate to the local hospitals for children in need, make your own dog toys, or stuff dog beds for a local shelter. My favorite toy recipes are included with the quilt recipes, and can help you reduce your fabric waste to ZERO. My trash can also came from the dollar store, and sits to the right of my cutting table. As I cut fabric, the scraps go in the bowl, the schnitzels go in the can to be used as stuffing. **What is a Schnitzel?** It's a piece of fabric that is too small to be used in scrap quilting. The narrowest strips I keep and use are 1¼" strips and the smallest squares I keep are 2" squares. Conversely, if I have more than ⅛ of a yard of fabric, I don't consider it to be a scrap. Instead, I put it in the section of my stash that is 'Up For Grabs.' This means that it is fabric that is not required for any pre-planned project and can be used as the need arises. This 'Up For Grabs' section is the first place I look for fabric to 'add in' or 'calm down' a scrappy quilt. Even ⅛ of a yard of fabric is enough to unify an entire quilt design.

-> Choose your 'standard sizes' based on the requirements of your favorite quilt books or patterns. My sizes are 2" squares, 2½" squares, 2 7/8" squares, 1¼" to 3" strips, random lengths, and 2½" x 40" strips. (Also, for flannel fabric only, I prefer 3" squares. See the note about flannel, included in the 'Standard Sizes' section.) Some of my standard sizes play with each other in my quilt recipes, others are easy to adapt to popular patterns.

-> Carve up your backlog of scraps as you feel inspired to. Make sure you do this in small batches. If you spend 4 days straight carving up scraps, you will be miserable for several reasons. First of all, too much fussy cutting gets BORING and overwhelming. (Trust me, I've done it. Learn from my mistakes.) Secondly, spending too many hours cutting in one session is very hard on your body, even if cutting is your FAVORITE part of quilting. The best way to avoid repetitive motion disorders and arthritis is to change activities frequently. When you do the same thing over and over, one set of bones, joints, and tendons does all the work for too long, and things become inflamed. (I'm not a medical professional, and if you are worried about your habits and activities talk to your doctor and/or get an assessment by a physical therapist. They can help you design the healthiest body mechanics for your set of tasks.) Even if you use the best ergonomic tools and the smartest and healthiest body mechanics you can, standing at a cutting board for twelve hours will give you a sore back. (Learn from my mistakes, people! I'm in my thirties, and I hobbled like I was an arthritic senior citizen the last time I binged on fussy cutting.)

Additionally, having a sharp rotary blade will make this task more pleasurable, and save you wear and tear on both your cutting mat and your body. This is because a sharp blade requires less strength/pressure and fewer repetitions of each cut. If your blade is sharp enough, you should only need one motion to make a cut.

Also, the sharper your blade, the more pieces of fabric you can cut with one motion. (Conversely, if your blade IS sharp, but you still have to go over each cut more than once, you are trying to cut too many layers of material.) While it faster to cut several pieces at once, it is important to find the right balance between cutting *accuracy* and efficiency. Cutting too many layers reduces the efficacy of your measurements, and makes edges, and thus your entire quilt, less neat.

-> When one of your bins of 'standard size' pieces fills up, make a quilt using those precuts. Like the bowl that visually signals that it is time to carve scraps, a full storage bin means that it is time to make a quilt and empty a storage container. If you simply get another container so that you can store more scraps, then you are reverting to your old habits of saving fabric to use 'someday'. Tsk, Tsk, Tsk! We are trying to clean out unused fabric, so don't fall into this trap. Another reason to use your homemade precuts as soon as your container is full is to keep your scrap stash current and your palate complimentary. Fabrics that are similar in age tend to match colors and styles more easily than fabric that has a variety of ages. Think about trying to match an 80's calico with a brand new piece of fabric. CLASH!!!! You can do it, and you can make it look good, but it takes a bit more work, and a bit more effort to design. (Hint: The uglier a piece of fabric is, the smaller you should cut it. Also, a little bit of ugly fabric will disappear into a large palate of beautiful fabric, which is another good reason to carve up your back log of scraps in small doses.)

How to Implement the ScrapStashtic System

Standard Sizes

These are the sizes that I use for the recipes included in this book. However, you could use any sizes that you would prefer so long as they are complementary. Keep in mind that the more scrap sizes you select, the more storage you will need and the longer it will take you to accumulate enough scraps to make a quilt.

My standard sizes

-> 2" squares: I either use these by themselves to make 4-patch, 9-patch, 25-patch, or postage stamp blocks, or to make Charm Quilts. I mix them with my 1¼" to 3" strips as the center of a wonky log cabin, or with my Jelly Roll strips for a traditional log cabin. I also use them as cornerstones for 2" sashing.

-> 2½" squares: These are in my favorite family of precuts! They play with Jelly Rolls and 2 7/8" squares and can be used in any patterns for Mini Charm Packs or Jelly Rolls. This size is one of my highest priorities when I am carving scraps because it is SO versatile.

-> 2 7/8" squares: This size of square makes half-square triangles that finish at 2½." I store my 'add-a-quarter inch' ruler right in this bin for convenience. These are also in my favorite family of precuts. They play with Jelly Rolls and 2½" squares and can be used in any patterns for Mini Charm Packs or Jelly Rolls. This size is another one of my highest priorities when I am carving scraps because it is also SO versatile. Look for places that you can substitute these units in precut Jelly Roll patterns.

Half-Square Triangle Tutorial:

There are many methods for making half-square triangle units, but this is my favorite for speed, neatness, and ease of execution.
-> Place two 2 7/8" squares, right sides together.
-> Mark a line on the diagonal with your favorite marking pen. I like a fine point permanent marker, or a cheap ball-point pen. I don't use a fancy marking pen or disappearing ink for this step because the line will be trimmed away.
-> Leaving a ¼" seam allowance, sew on either side of the diagonal line.
-> Cut on the diagonal line, then press the two half-square triangle units open.

These units are very versatile and can be mixed into almost any quilt recipe in this book.

ScrapStashtic Quilts

> ### *Side Note About Quilt-As-You-Go/Stitch-And-Flip Technique:*
> This is a good technique if you do not have access to a long-arm or mid-arm quilting machine. Instead of piecing the entire quilt top before sewing it to the batting and quilt back, it allows you to quilt through all three layers of the 'quilt sandwich' as you piece the quilt top.
>
> You can learn more about this technique from a number of books, classes, and internet resources. There are also a number of specialty tools and rulers available to make your stitch-and-flip projects neater.

-> Random-width strips, 1¼" to 3" wide, of random length, 2" to 40" long: This is the box that fills up the fastest for me. When the box is full, I sort the strips roughly by length. Sometimes, I sew the strips into 'fabric' and use the 'fabric' to make Coin blocks or cut 'light' or 'dark' squares from the scrappy fabric to use in bigger patterns. Other times, I use the random strips to make a wobbly version of a French braid, although there is a LOT of waste from this method. If I have an abundance of very short, random-width strips, I build wonky log cabins around a 2" square. If I have an abundance of strips approximately six inches and lots of batting scraps, I like to use these scraps for quilt-as-you-go/stitch-and-flip techniques.

-> 2½" wide x 40" long strips: These are homemade Jelly Roll strips that run from selvedge to selvedge in length. (If the strips are not long enough, they get added to the random width strip box, above.) I love this size because there are so many patterns for Jelly Rolls. These are also in my favorite family of precuts. They play with Mini Charm Squares (2½") and 2 7/8" squares, and can be used in any patterns for Mini Charm Packs or Jelly Rolls. This size is another one of my highest priorities when I am carving scraps because it is SO versatile. When I have an overabundance of this size, I like to use a Jelly Roll Race variation to use up a lot of fabric, very quickly. My favorite variation is one that I came up with, the 'Jelly Roll Race Log Cabin'. (I still haven't seen anyone else make this quilt yet, so check it out in the recipe section!) They also work very well with French braid quilts and a few specialty rulers.

How to Implement the ScrapStashtic System

-> 3" Flannel Squares: I chose 3" squares for my flannel scraps so that they couldn't accidentally get mixed in with my other precut sizes. I use these precuts exclusively for charity quilts, and the larger size means that the blocks knock together much more quickly.

->Scraps: Fussy cut your scraps as they fill your scrap bowl, and place your pre-cuts in their storage bins.

->Stash Annex: I carve up anything smaller than 1/8 of a yard and anything that is oddly shaped, like the scraps from an appliqué project. Anything larger than 1/8 of a yard, but not claimed for a specified project goes in my 'stash annex'.

There are three sections in my stash annex:

1) Up For Grabs: These are the pieces that are smaller than one yard but larger than 1/8 of a yard, and are perfect for unifying a scrappy quilt. Sometimes they are the focus square in a block, sometimes I use them for 'light' or 'dark' to calm down a scrappy quilt.

2) Dominators: Pieces of fabric that are larger than a yard can serve as the 'light' or 'dark' in a larger quilt or can serve as the sashing. If there are several yards of a fabric available, you can use the scraps as accent fabric or let your quilt highlight that one special print. In other words, this print can be in one large piece, or cut up and incorporated as small squares throughout a scrap quilt, or both. When used as small pieces, it can tie scraps that are very different together into one idea. Quilt patterns with large swathes of white fabric adapt well to this technique.

3) Almost a Quilt: This section is the bridge between my scrap annex and the heart of my stash. This is where I keep 'fat quarter bundles' and collections of 'medium whole scraps' from larger quilts. These small collections will definitely

Side Note About Flannel:

I cut my flannel scraps into (what I consider to be) a very unusual size. As a result, my 3" flannel squares do not 'play' with any of my other precut scraps. THIS IS ABSOLUTELY INTENTIONAL! Just in case I am designing quilts before I have my morning coffee, the size of the flannel squares serves as a reminder that flannel ONLY plays with flannel.

When working with flannel scraps, I make 4-patch or 9-patch blocks and put them together with plain blocks or 3" sashing, depending on how much 'calm down' flannel I have on hand. ('Calm down fabric' is explained later on, in the 'Overall Guidelines' section.)

Since this is all that I do with flannel scraps, this is the only place I mention flannel in the entire book. So, allow me to add this one additional recommendation:

If flannel is your specialty, make sure that you are extra nice to your sewing machine. Clean and lightly oil your machine with EVERY bobbin change because flannel is very fuzzy/linty and will increase wear on your machine. (Nice, new, computerized machines with plastic gears are particularly vulnerable to flannel fuzz.)

need additional fabric to make a quilt, but they are a great start, just waiting for the inspiration to become an artistic statement.

Choosing YOUR standard sizes:

I have given an extensive explanation of the precut sizes I make, and the benefits of each. My ScrapStashtic system is built around the sizes that I use, however, you can implement my system using any sizes that you like. When deciding on your own set of sizes, look at your patterns and books. Do you make a lot of quilts that play around with 3", 6", and 10" squares? Do you like a 10" finished block so that you can mix in precut Layer Cakes? (Also called Piece of Cake, Dimes, or Quilt Patties) Do you use 5" squares and make tossed 9-patches? Are 1" postage stamp quilts your favorite thing ever? Let your existing quilting habits guide you as you select your personal standard sizes if you choose to adapt my system.

What is considered ridiculously small?

As you implement the ScrapStashtic System, you will spend enough time fussy cutting that you will develop an 'eye' for roughly measuring fabric. At a glance, you will be able to judge what squiggly piece of fabric can be carved into one of your set sizes.

Assuming that you have already selected your precut standard sizes, you will also need to decide what fabric is too small to mess with, and what fabric is too large to waste in a scrap collection. For me, fabric that is smaller than ⅛ of a yard, but is not part of a small corresponding, complementary collection is perfect for carving up into precuts. Also, I fussy cut any irregular scraps, like the leftovers from an appliqué project. If it is larger than ⅛ of a yard of fabric, I store the fabric as part of my stash to 'add in' to my scrappy quilts as I design them.

You will also need to decide which precuts are your favorites. My priority is 2½" x 40" strips, and anything that will play with them. Accordingly, my second choice are 2½" squares, and my third choice are 2 7/8" squares. The easiest precuts to make are the random strips because they have the widest set of criteria and most scraps can adapt to fit my requirements. If you are using your own set of sizes, you will have to assess the best way to fit your scrapping needs based on your personal preferences.

Once your parameters are defined, you will develop the ability to quickly decide which scrap will most easily suit each of your standard-sized precuts. Initially, you may have to measure and consider each piece of fabric you are planning to carve, and your decision making process will seem slow and cumbersome. As you gain experience (and nothing can substitute for experience) your decision making process will speed up. During this process, you will sometimes make decisions that you will second guess as soon as you make a cut. Relax, and remind yourself to be forgiving. After all, why quibble over a quarter of an inch of fabric, when you would have thrown out the whole scrap before?

How to Implement the ScrapStashtic System

Organizing your thoughts....

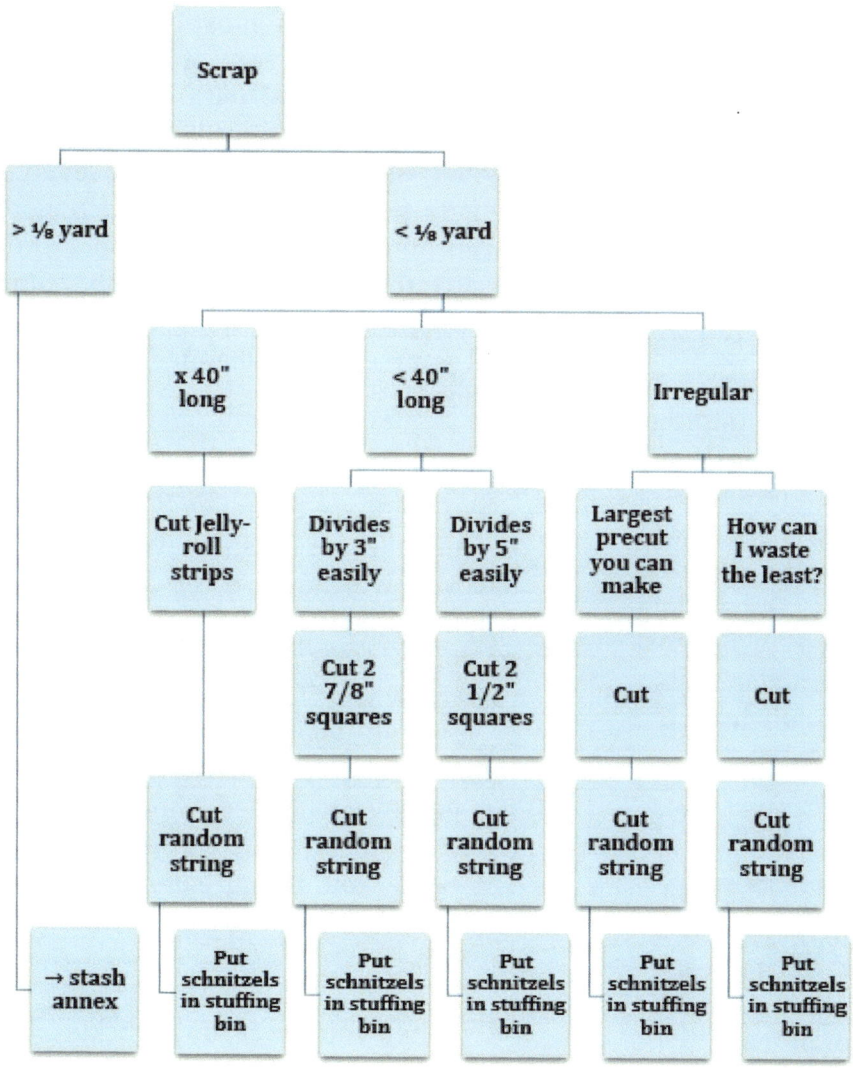

If this flow chart confuses you, don't worry about it at all. Your brain will develop a decision making process of its own as you gain experience. I included this chart as a 'picture' of how I think when I am carving up scraps. It will either really help you, or be completely incomprehensible. I find that I can't understand other people's decision charts until I have had experience making the same types of choices. Consider this 'picture' as entertainment and completely ancillary if the information is unappealing in this format. This is a construct of the information already provided within the text of this book.

This Image is Also Available on my Website to Print:

I would not only like to grant readers permission to print the image of this flow chart, but I actually strongly ENCOURAGE it! If this chart helps your cognitive process, I recommend you print it to hang in your sewing room. Please see the web address below to find a printable version, right there on my website. If you decide to use different precut sizes, you can draw your own flow chart to fit the needs of your own decision-making process, or use the blank version I have included.

http://www.janelleamacbeth.website/excerpts.html

How to Organize Your Scraps, and Use Them Continually

Each precut size will need its own storage container with a lid to keep the dust out of your fabric. The boxes should be roughly the size of a shoebox, so that your entire stash of homemade precuts takes up a relatively small amount of storage space. All of my precuts, (except for the 2½" x 40" strips) fit on one half of a shelf. My stash and my stash annex fit in one dresser drawer. By limiting the amount of space I am willing to dedicate to unplanned projects, I manage to keep a high turnover rate in my fabric collections and finish what I start.

Storage Rules

- Choose small boxes with lids for each set of precut scraps.
- Carve scraps into precuts as the scrap bowl fills up from finishing your other quilt projects.
- When a box is full, make a quilt that will use those precuts. Your goal is to empty the box as much as possible.

Clearing the Backlog

If you are like most quilters, there is a deep dark corner of your quilting space that is filled with leftovers and scraps from old projects that you should use 'someday'. Or, once your friends hear that you are starting to scrap quilt, they will bring you THEIR scraps to deal with. At some point, regardless of whose fault it is, you will find yourself overwhelmed with older scraps.

It is very easy to get frustrated when there are too many bins of fabric. It feels like the scraps never end, and like you will never catch up with the amount of sewing crossing your table, no matter what you do. This is the time to narrow your focus to what is in front of you, and what needs your attention immediately. If a backlog of scraps has you overwhelmed, choose the one container of scraps to work with that will give you the greatest sense of satisfaction, and then work ONLY from this bin.

When you are ready to tackle a bin of fabric scraps, work ONLY from this bin, in small batches until it is empty. (Remember, too much cutting at one time has nasty side effects.) Here's an important tip: Only pull out as many scraps as you can work with RIGHT NOW. Chances are, if your backlog is years old, it has settled into a mellow, compressed state from waiting to be used. If you go through it all at the start of your anti-backlog project, several things will happen. First of all, you will overestimate how quickly you can reach your goal, which sets you up for the disappointment of watching a completely arbitrary (but seemingly important) deadline whiz right past. Secondly, the fabric that you touch, fondle, sort, and straighten will fluff up, and will not fit back into its original container. This will also contribute to the sensation of being buried in fabric.

The only time you should sort your backlog of fabric BEFORE you start carving your scraps into precuts is when your fabric is a mixture of yardage and scraps.

Why Quilt for Charity?

Have you ever heard of the monks who make beautiful sand mandalas while they meditate? They spend hours creating breathtaking artwork. While they work, they are filled with the joy of creating, and the peace of meditation. When they are finished with their designs, the monks sweep up the colored sand that they use in the mandalas and destroy the artwork. In silence, they walk the dust of their lost art to the river, and pour it in. They do this so that the peace and beauty that they have created will spread into the world.

Charity quilting is our equivalent of the artwork created by these monks. While we are sewing, we are creating peace and joy for ourselves, and when we bring our finished quilts to the charity of our choice, we are releasing that peace and beauty to continue its work in the world without us.

There are a variety of charities that accept quilts as donations, and they fill many different needs. Some charities exist to spread the healing love of quilts to people who need emotional support, such as cancer patients, returning soldiers, those dealing with grief and loss, and more. Other charities exist to fill the practical need for quilts.

I love charity quilting for both reasons. I love the idea of sending peace and love into the world to work for the forces of good and happiness. More than anything, however, I love the creative freedom that is conferred when I am making charity quilts for practical needs.

Every once in a while, you wind up with a quilt that is just...plug-ugly. And that's cool. The world needs quilts to keep people warm. This is a very reassuring thought because there is a point in almost every quilt when I am convinced that THIS quilt is going to be the ugliest thing going. Time after time, I am proved wrong. The vast majority of the scrappy quilts that I make are stunning, appealing, or fascinating. Once in a while, I produce one that is beautiful. Or pretty. But, at the darkest hour of every quilt, I need to be able to remind myself that even if THIS quilt turns out ugly, it will still be able to keep someone warm.

If scrappy quilting still seems like a risky artistic statement, remember that others have different definitions of beauty, and that there will always be someone in the world who is grateful to be warm.

Quilt Recipes

I call the projects in this book Quilt Recipes instead of Quilt Patterns because I am not giving you a set of directions to make one particular quilt. These directions are more like your chili recipe or your mother-in-law's meatloaf. Yes, somewhere in a cookbook, there exists an exact set of directions for how to make a perfect meatloaf, or a gourmet pot of chili. Mostly, however, these dishes are made within the guidelines of a few techniques, and ultimately, are based on what you have in the pantry.

The quilts in this book are based on general guidelines and formulas, but you will need to adjust my recommendations based on what you have on hand. No two scrap quilts that I make are ever the same, and I almost never follow a pattern without changing something to suit my needs. When it comes to adding your own creativity to the Quilt Recipes that follow, you may or may not want to draw on the design concepts I provide in the next chapter. Let your creativity flow! There are no wrong answers here, and you can always donate the ugly quilts to someone who is cold.

4-Patch Recipes

Sew 4 squares into a block. Squares can be 2" or 2½", and can be all scrappy, or scrappy with a focus fabric.

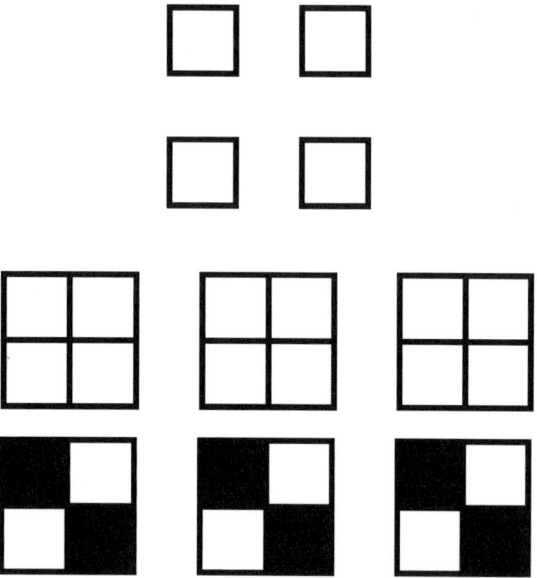

Blocks can be assembled into tops with sashing…

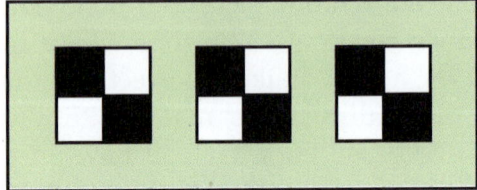

…sashing with cornerstones…

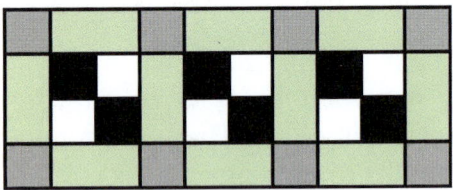

…or with plain blocks that are the same size as the pieced blocks.
Quilt layouts can be random, streak of lightning…

…variations of the 'round the world' pattern such as this one…

…or this one…

Quilt Recipes

...stripy quilted into columns...

...or a variation of 4-patch with adapted rail fence:

Variation1: Rows 1 and 2 repeated inversely

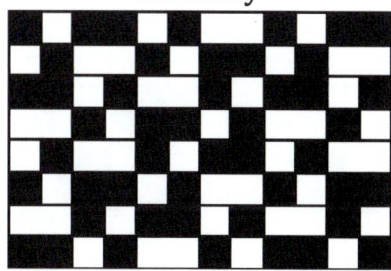

Variation 2: Rows 1 and 2 repeated exactly

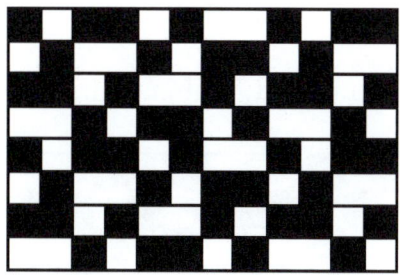

9-Patch Recipes

Sew nine squares into a block, 3 squares x 3 squares. Squares can be 2" or 2½", and can be all scrappy or scrappy with a focus fabric.

31

ScrapStashtic Quilts

Blocks can be arranged in light and dark patterns around a center square...

...split light and dark with half square triangles (from the 2 7/8" precuts),...

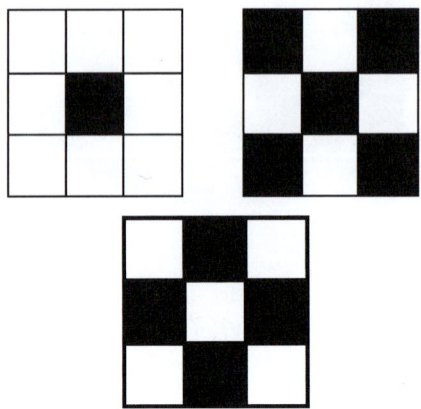

...rail fence and combinations thereof...

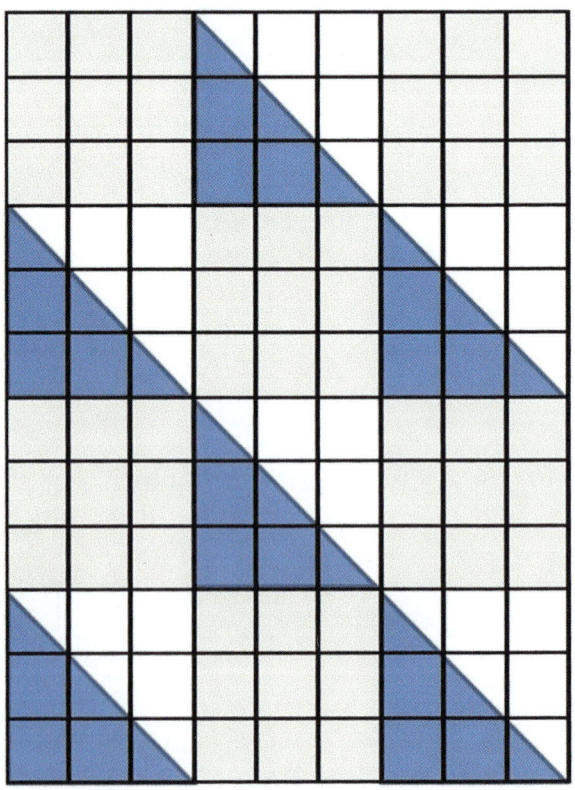

Quilt Recipes

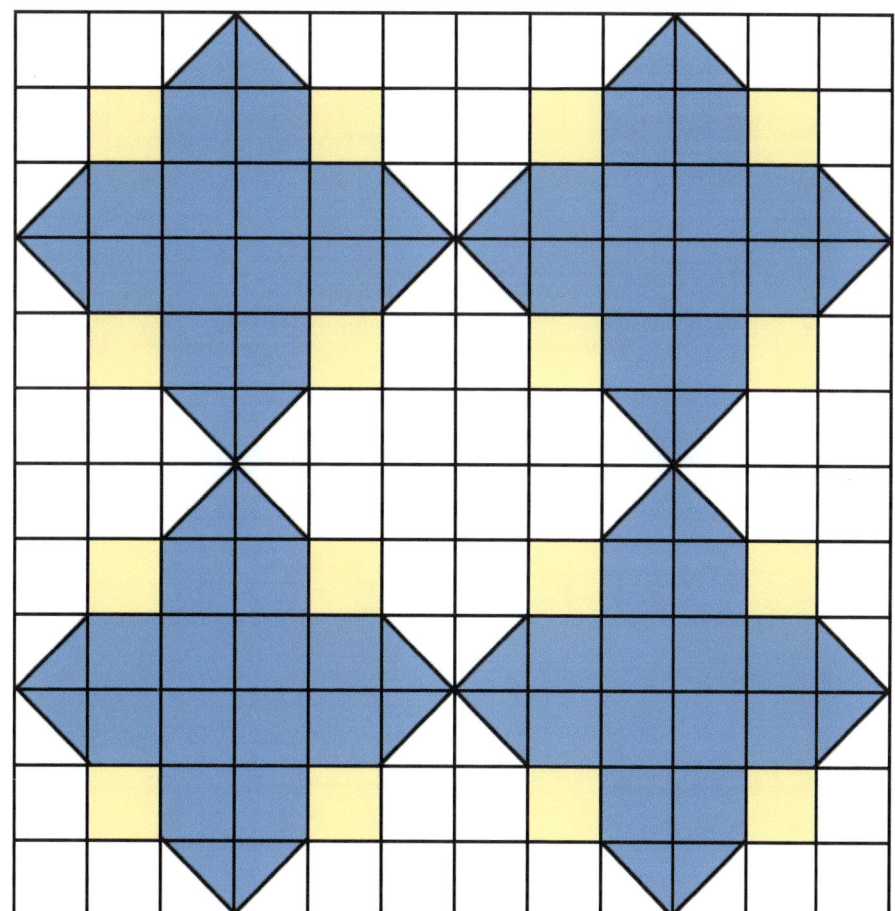

33

ScrapStashtic Quilts

...or cut into four squares and re-sewn into a tossed 9-patch.

34

Quilt Recipes

Blocks can be assembled into tops with sashing, sashing with cornerstones, or plain blocks that are the same size as the pieced blocks, just like for the 4-patch. There are countless possibilities!

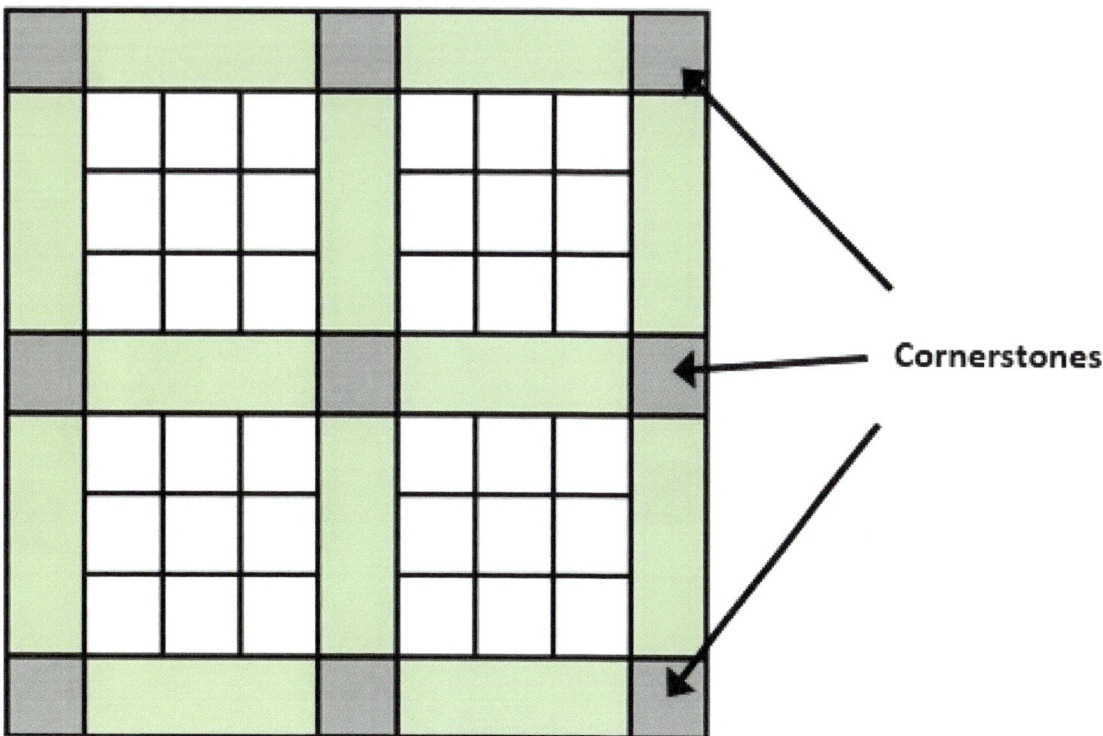

Cornerstones

ScrapStashtic Quilts

25-Patch Recipes

Sew 25 squares into a block, 5 squares by 5 squares.

...light and dark around the center square, or mixed with half square triangles from 2 7/8" squares.

Squares can be 2" or 2½", and can be all scrappy, scrappy with a center square...

36

Quilt Recipes

Also, scrappy blocks can be cut in half on the diagonal and reassembled with a large focus fabric in a half square triangle block...

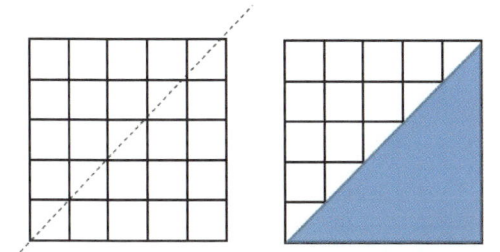

...or you can assemble two of the blocks shown above into two large bowtie units.

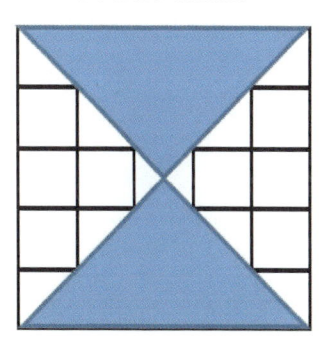

Bowtie Tutorial:

To make a bowtie square, place two squares, right sides together. Mark a line on the diagonal with your favorite marking pen. Leaving a ¼" seam allowance, sew on either side of the diagonal line. Cut on the diagonal line, then press the two half-square triangle units open. (Please note: the steps thus far create a half-square triangle unit.)

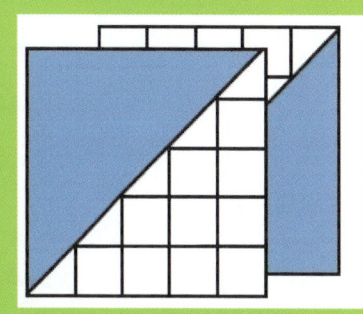

Then take two of these half-square triangle units and again place them right sides together, specifically oriented so that the each light triangle is touching a dark triangle, as shown below. (The squares should be lined up corner to corner. They are only off set in these diagrams to demonstrate orientation of the triangles.)

Then use the following diagram to complete the steps listed below:

- First, mark on the dotted line.
- Sew on the solid lines, leaving a ¼" seam allowance.
- Then cut on the marked line.

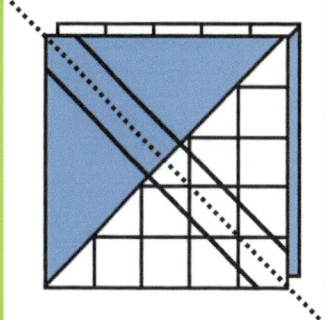

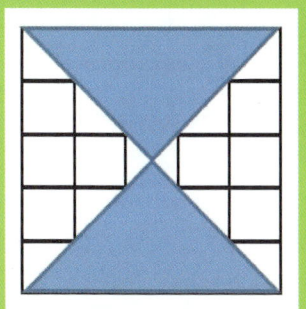

These directions make two finished units. These blocks are very versatile and can be mixed into almost any quilt recipe in this book.

ScrapStashtic Quilts

Check out these other cool patterns/recipes:

Don't forget, blocks can be assembled into tops with sashing or sashing with cornerstones. The section regarding cornerstones can be found at the end of the recipes section.

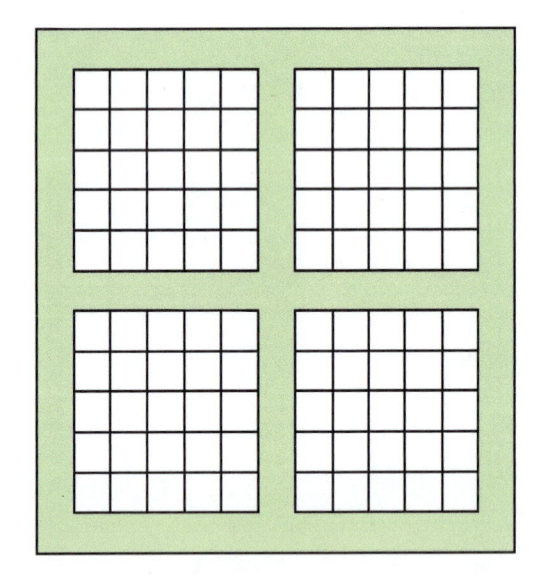

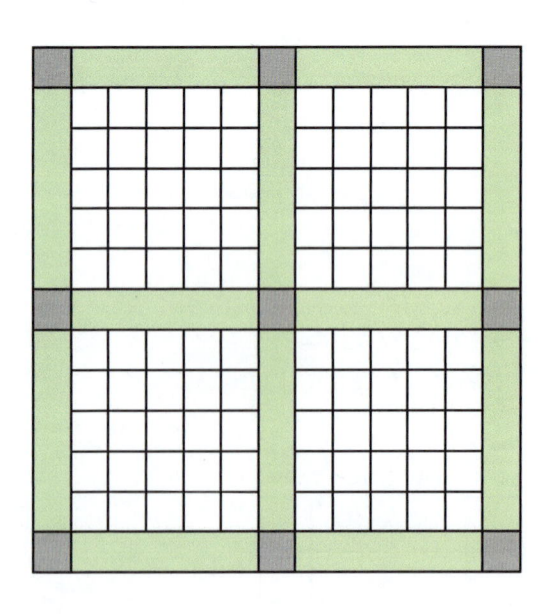

38

5 by 7 Patch Recipes

Sew squares into rectangular blocks, 5 squares by 7 squares.

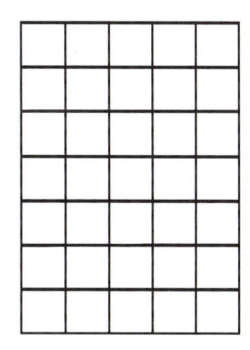

Squares can be 2" or 2½", or be made of half square triangle units from the 2 7/8" squares. This block can be scrappy, light and dark, or streak of lightning.

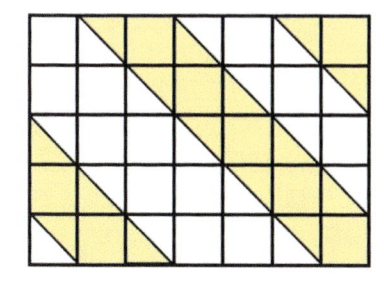

Blocks and sashing can be assembled into tops with or without cornerstones...

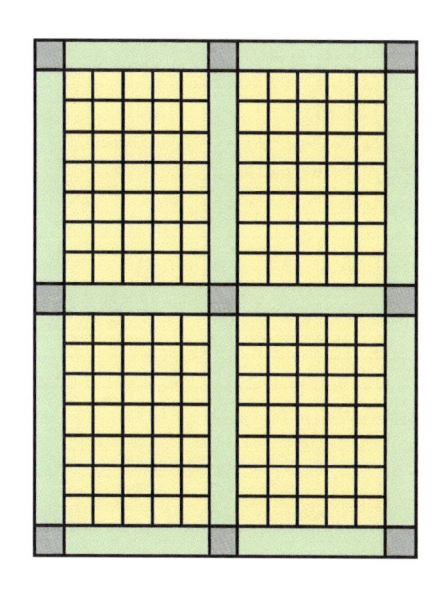

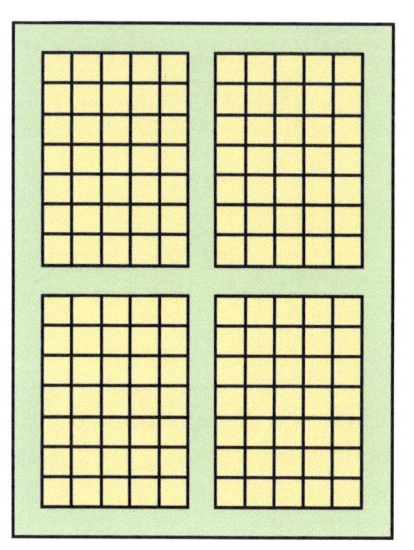

However, BE AWARE of the size and shape of your finished quilt as you play with these recipes.

ScrapStashtic Quilts

...and you can play around with the orientation of the blocks for a unique look.

Coins and Variations

Sew strips together into a whole piece of 'fabric', and then cut it into blocks. You can use random-width strips or 2½" x 40" strips, either all scrappy, or light and dark...

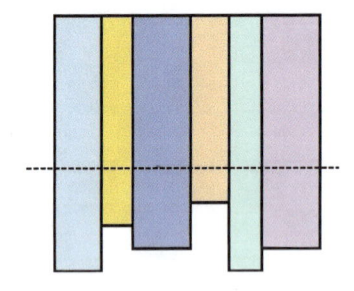

Blocks can be rectangular or square. When planning your rectangular blocks, keep in mind that a ratio of approximately ⅓ to ⅔ has a strong visual appeal. Examples of block sizes using this ratio include 5" by 7½", 6" by 9", and 10" by 15". (I use 6" by 9" for my rectangular blocks, and 10" by 10" for my square blocks.)

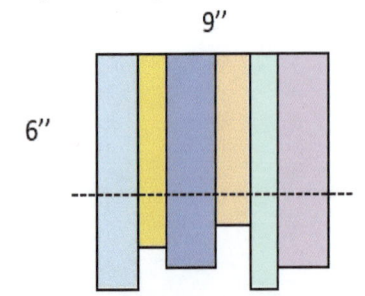

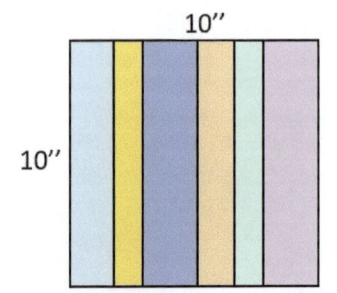

Quilt Recipes

These squares and rectangles can have any of the permutations done to regular squares and rectangles. Square blocks can have a solid triangle added to opposing corners to add a bowtie, and both squares and rectangles can be cut in half on the diagonal and reassembled with a large focus fabric in a half square triangle block.

Check out some of these cool ideas:

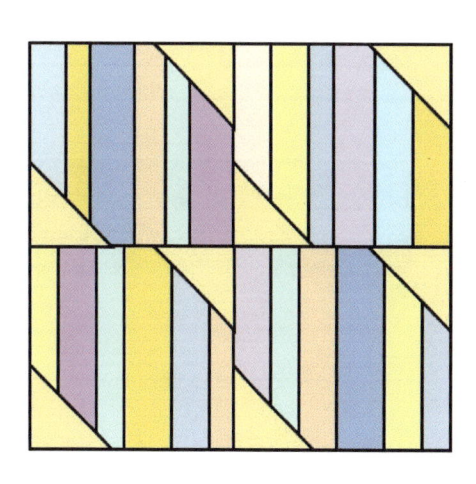

41

ScrapStashtic Quilts

Blocks can be assembled into tops with sashing or sashing with cornerstones.

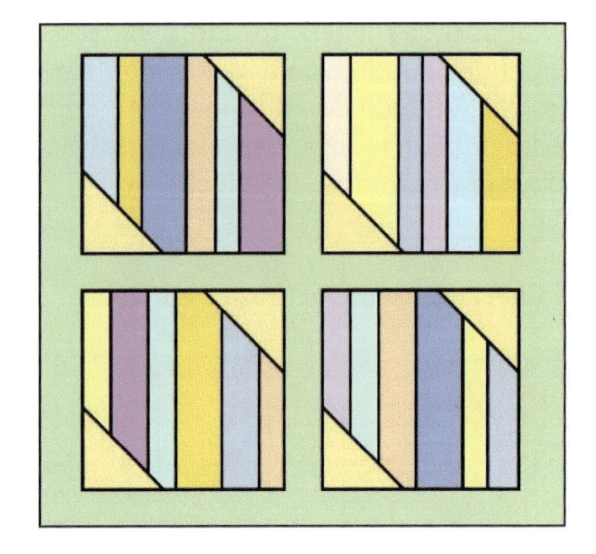

Keep in mind that your blocks are being made from your scraps, so each block will be unique and interesting!

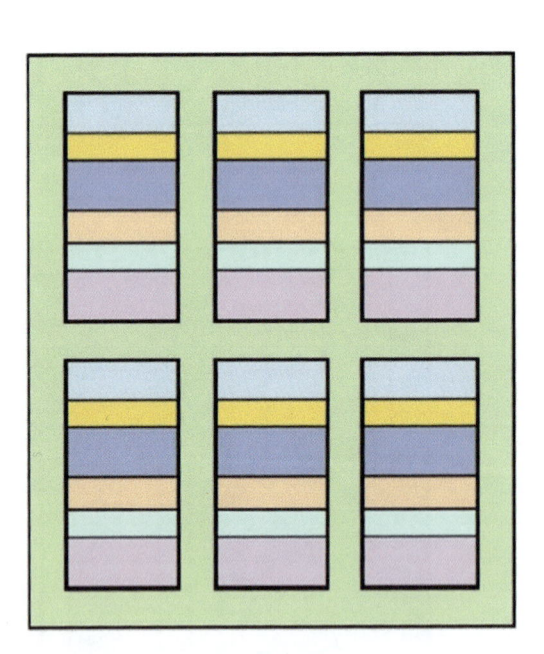

Quilt Recipes

Log Cabin and Variations

Make a log cabin block around a center square. There are two primary ways of doing this: Log Cabin and Wonky Log Cabin.

For regular Log Cabin blocks, you would use 2½" squares for the center squares, and 2½" x 40" strips for the 'logs'. You can use all scrappy, or light and dark fabrics.

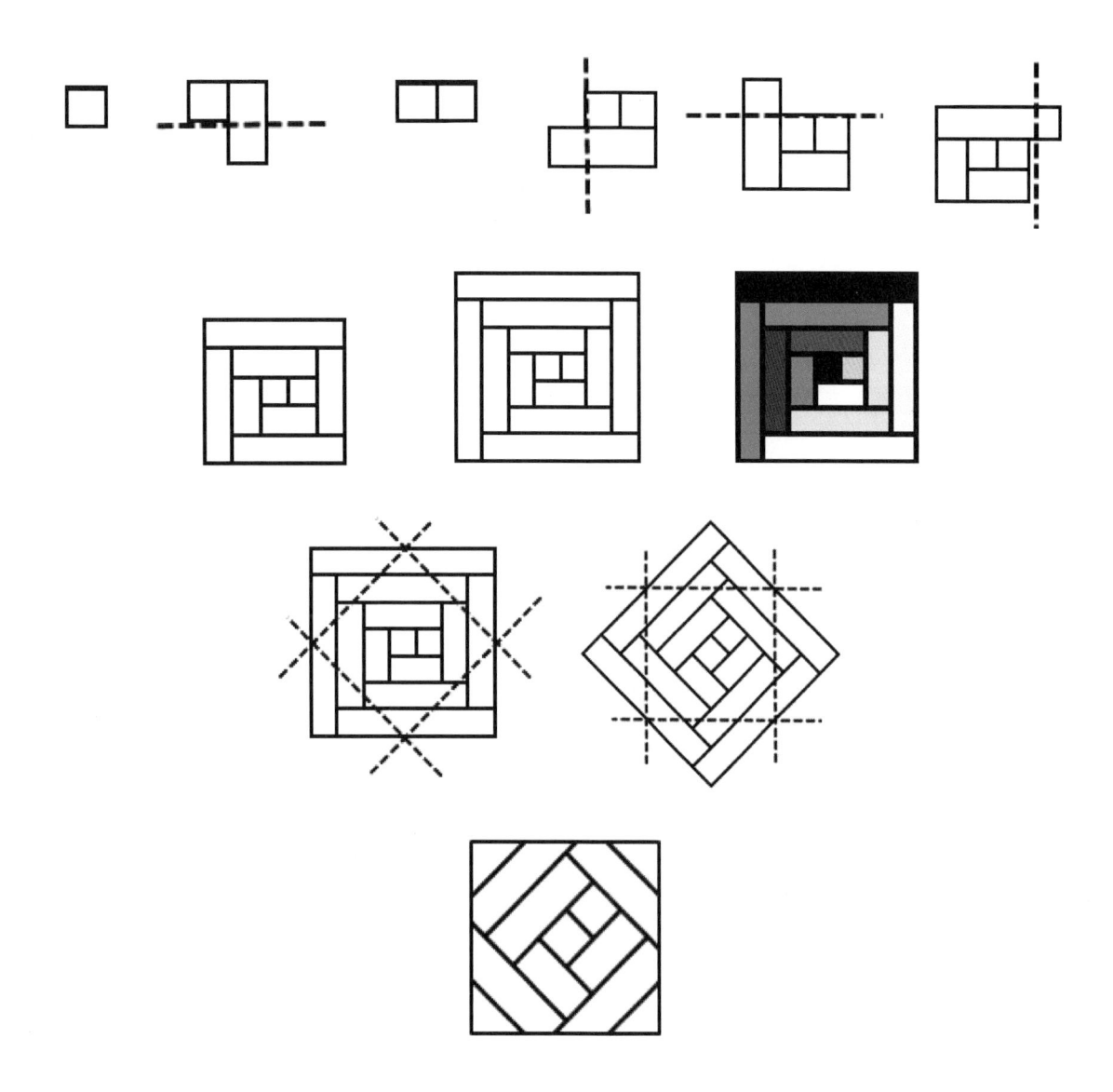

43

ScrapStashtic Quilts

For Wonky Log Cabin blocks, you would use 2" or 2½" squares for the center squares, and random-width strips for the 'logs'. You can use all scrappy, or light and dark fabrics.

Because the strips are random-width, the center square often ends up off-center. If the sides are particularly uneven, you may end up adding strips to just the top and bottom, or to just the two sides, in order to make it more square.

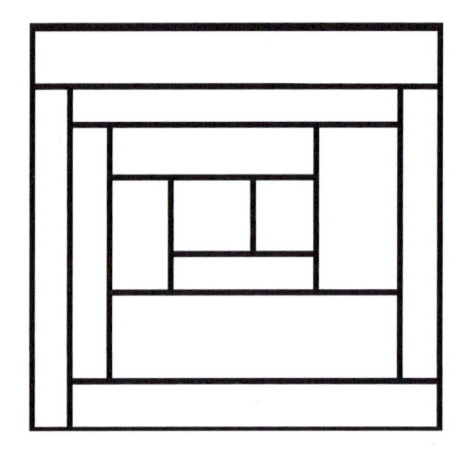

Square up the blocks before assembling!

Quilt layouts for both the regular Log Cabin and the Wonky Log Cabin can be random, streak of lightning, 'round the world, or stripy quilted into columns. Blocks can be assembled into tops with sashing or sashing with cornerstones.

44

Quilt Recipes

Jelly Roll Race Log Cabin

Jelly Roll Race quilts are very popular right now. There are tutorial videos all over the internet. In case you have missed this creative fad, I highly recommend looking up a video or two.

I have created my own variation of the Jelly Roll Race. This is my go-to quilt when I need super-speed in the sewing room. Basically, you start a Jelly Roll Race quilt, but turn it into a quilt-sized log cabin square!

For this project, I am assuming that you are using your own, home-cut Jelly Roll strips, so you will need to choose either 42 or 84 strips (2½" x 40") that play well together. 42 strips will make a large lap quilt, and 84 will make a small queen-sized quilt. Sew them together either in the normal, end to end method OR in the method of piecing a binding. The end to end method is depicted first:

End-to-End Method

String together either 42 or 84 strips (2½" by 40") in the following manner, with a normal quarter inch seam allowance:

Etc...

(Keep in mind that even though this step takes forever, when you finish it you are actually halfway done with the quilt!)

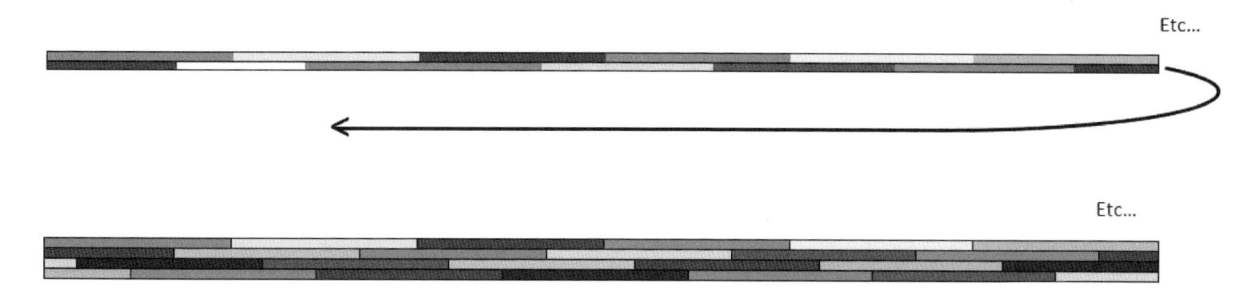

Etc...

Etc...

45

ScrapStashtic Quilts

Binding Method

String together either 42 or 84 strips (2½" by 40") in the following manner. Sew on the diagonal as shown below, then cut off the triangle-shaped excess from both pieces, leaving a ¼" seam allowance.

(The solid line represents where to sew, and the dotted line represents where to cut.)

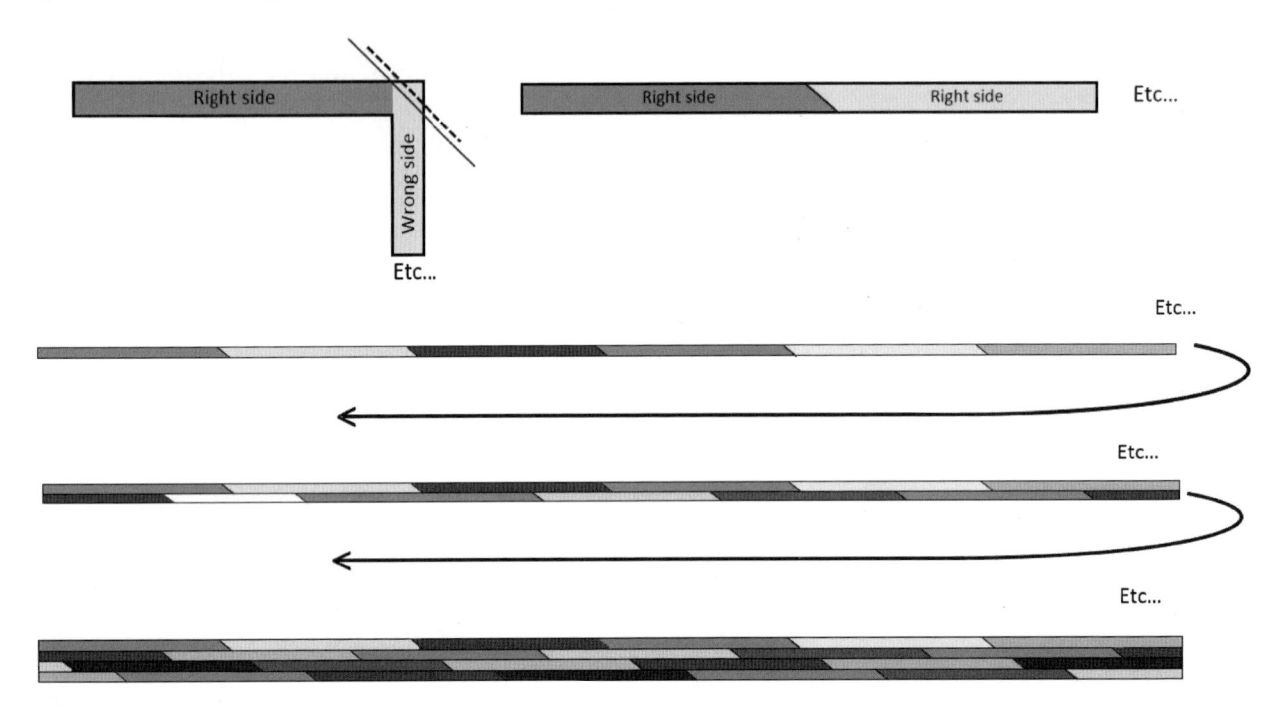

Creating the Log Cabin

Once you have the desired train that is four strips wide, use the train to create one large, quilt-sized log cabin block.

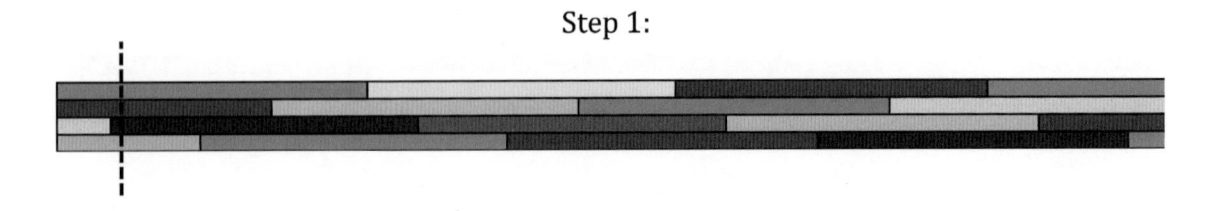

Step 1:

Quilt Recipes

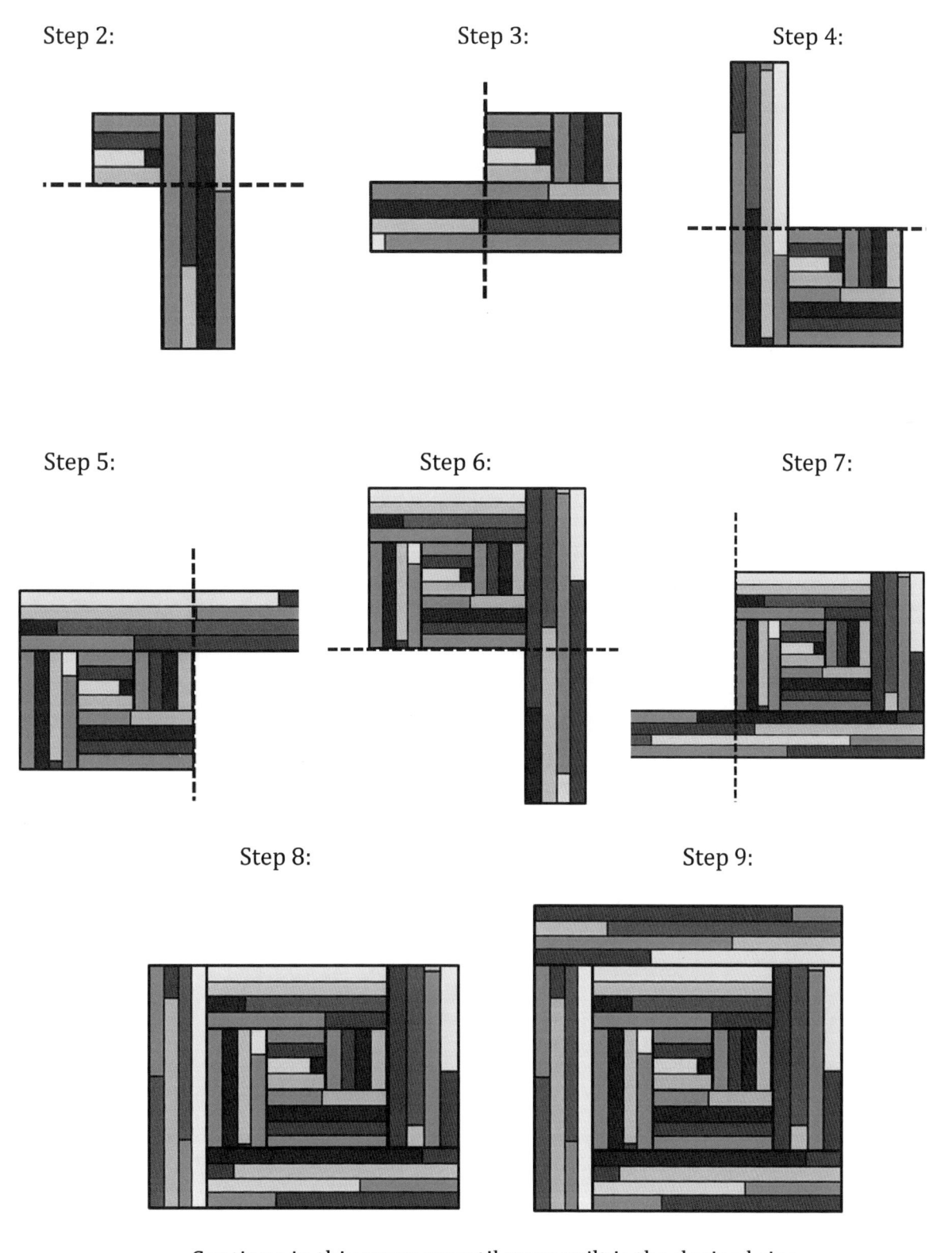

Step 2:

Step 3:

Step 4:

Step 5:

Step 6:

Step 7:

Step 8:

Step 9:

Continue in this manner until your quilt is the desired size.

47

ScrapStashtic Quilts

Variations

For any of these light and dark variations, use 42 Jelly Roll strips of a dark color to make one train, and 42 of a light color to make another train. Then alternate which train you are using according to the recipe:

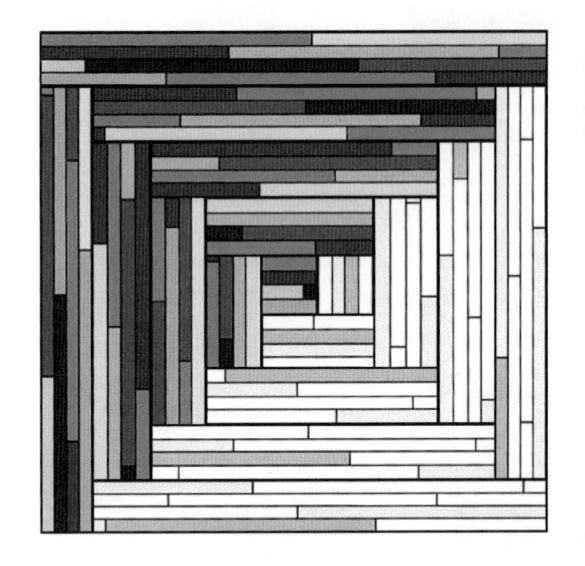

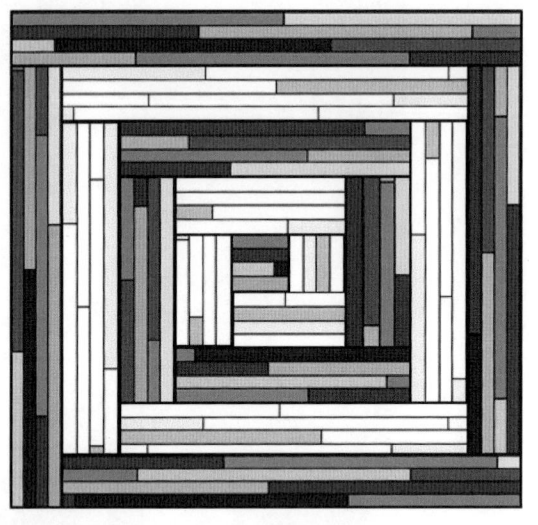

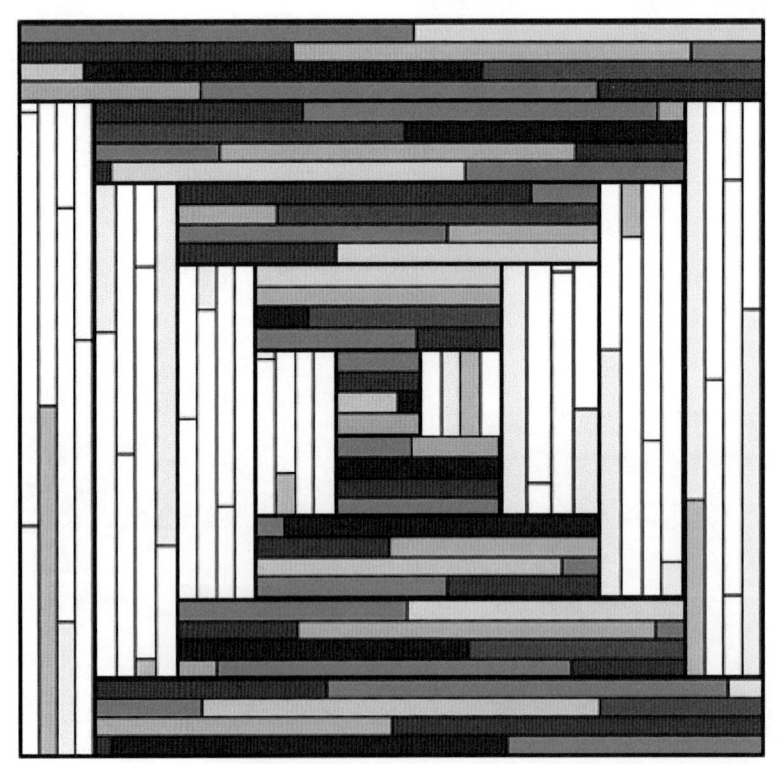

48

Cornerstones

Cornerstones are an excellent way to add a couple of hours of sewing to your quilting project. I LOVE cornerstones. First of all, cornerstones can really add a 'pop' to traditional quilt patterns. They also make the finished quilt MUCH NEATER, because smaller pieces of fabric between seams ultimately means less stretch in the finished quilt top. Most of all, though, I love cornerstones because of the endless variety they can add to quilt tops. Cornerstones are usually made of a plain square, but they can be replaced by any small unit that has the correct finished size as your sashing. Check out the variations shown below. They can be added to almost any quilt top in this book. The possibilities are truly limitless!

These are just a few variations. Feel free to create your own, but keep in mind that the size of your cornerstones dictates the size of your sashing.

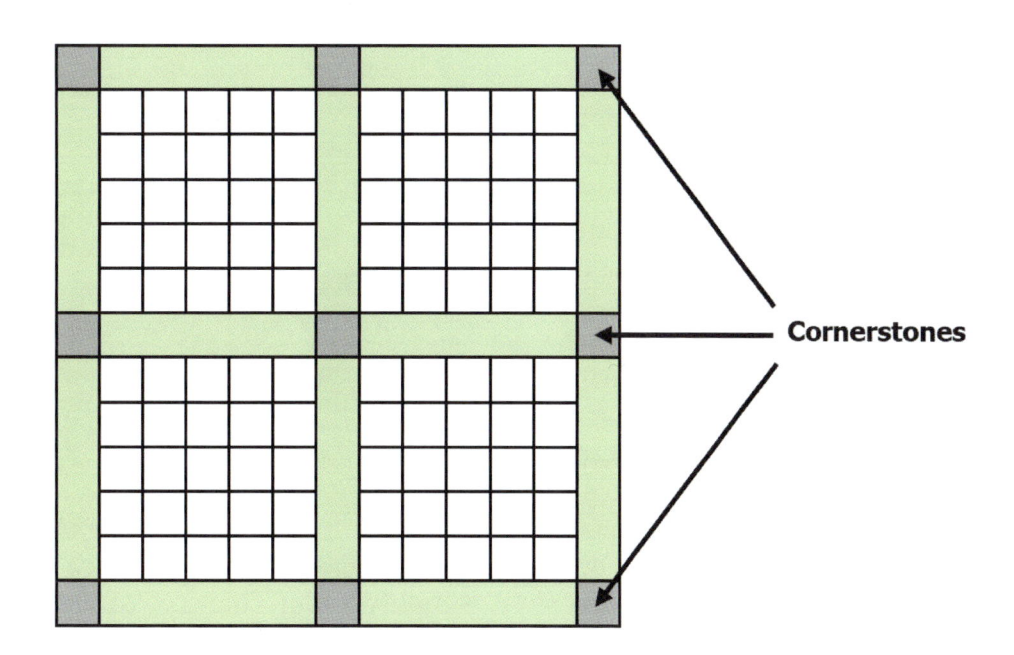

Cornerstones

Overall Design Guidelines

One of the most life-changing classes I took in college was a two-dimensional design class for freshman art majors. We spent the entire semester gluing pieces of black construction paper to white sketch paper. Sounds like kindergarten, right? The hands on experience and the intuitive design skills that I gained in that class are invaluable in my daily life as a quilter.

If you are interested in mimicking modern art in your quilting, or are looking to expand upon the quilt recipes found in this book, try simplifying the design ideas while you are in the planning stages. Use white and black unprinted paper to test out design ideas you have.

If you are interested in designing your own variation on a traditional block, try using 2" x 2" multicolored sticky notes to test your design ideas before you start sewing. (To make a half square triangle out of post it notes, layer two sticky notes of contrasting colors on top of each other. Then, fold the top sticky note in half along the diagonal.) I like to lay out my paper blocks on the dining room table, but if I need to keep my design as a pattern, I transfer the sticky notes to a piece of scrap book paper or poster board. Then, I can either take a picture of it, or pin my model to the wall behind my sewing machine to copy in fabric.

If you are experimenting with different ways to assemble your blocks into a quilt top, there are three ways to build a model of your quilt. To make sure that the blocks look good together, I like to build 4 sticky note models and place them on 4 square pieces of paper. Then, I can find the most pleasing arrangement of directional blocks. The second is to draw it, and color in the blocks to get a better idea of how the fabric color fits together, similar to the graphics in this book. The third is, of course, to lay the pieced blocks on a design wall, clean floor, or spare bed. Depending on how diverse your scrap fabric is, this is often the only way to find the best arrangement of your blocks.

To play with light/dark designs, simplify your blocks to black and white construction paper or large multicolored sticky notes. Find the arrangement that works best for you, and then take a picture of your design plan.

When designing my scrappy quilts from my precut scraps, I often allow the amount of focus fabric that I have to dictate the size of my quilt. The number of blocks I have when the fabric is gone ultimately determines how large my quilt is and whether it will be square or rectangular. The size and layout of the quilt will help me decide between using sashing, plain blocks, a 'white' field, floating/framing the blocks, or placing the blocks on point. The amount of fabric I have available for finishing will often help structure my choices regarding cornerstones, borders, backing, and binding.

Fabric Design Vocabulary

Background: the color of the fabric before it is printed

Ground: the small, low contrast designs that are printed on the background fabric. White on White prints usually consist of white fabric, printed with a white ground. Medium and large scale prints often have a ground 'behind' them to unify the large elements within the design.

Medium scale prints: Designs that range in size from a US Quarter to a US Half-dollar. Often medium scale prints 'float' over a low contrast ground.

Large scale prints: Designs that are larger than a US Half-dollar coin in size. Often large scale prints 'float' over a small or medium sized ground.

Border print: Fabric that has a large scale design along one selvage. Border fabric can add a unique look to the back of a quilt, or can be cut apart and used as two contrasting pieces of fabric in a quilt top.

Density: The density of a print describes how close together or far apart the designs are. The term can be applied to grounds or prints.

How to (Mostly) Avoid Making Ugly Quilts

There are several strategies to help you avoid making REALLY ugly scrap quilts. (Don't be afraid to experiment, though. Push your boundaries, and try something you wouldn't normally dare!)

-> Add a LARGE chunk of 'calm down fabric.' Up to 60% of the fabric in your scrappy quilt can be purchased for this specific quilt. By having the scrappy pieces serve as a contrasting 'pop' of color, your quilt will look more designed, and less like a poverty-hobby. When using large swathes of 'calm down fabric' within a quilt, I like a medium to large print with a lot of open space. When using large quantities of small pieces of 'calm down fabric,' I like a smaller design with a busy ground behind them. Some very reliable color palates in the 'calm down fabric' family include maroons, blues, turquoises, and brown. Printed blacks are also very dependable as 'calm down fabrics,' and white on white prints can work as well. I recommend waiting to use white-on-white prints until you get more comfortable designing your scrap quilt variations. Stay away from solid black, unless you want your quilt to look either Amish or VERY modern. Also stay away from solid white unless you are using 1930's or 1950's reproduction fabric for your blocks.

-> Add 2-3 pieces of purpose-purchased fabric from a single line of fabric. Using multiple pieces of fabric from the same design line will help you keep the statement of your quilt consistent, but will also push you closer to making quilts that are 100% scrappy. (The goal is not necessarily to wean you away from buying fabric to add to your scrappy quilts. The goal is to push your artistic boundaries so that you are fluent at improvising variations on traditional designs.) Quilts from this category can be anywhere from 40%-60% composed of fabric purchased for this purpose.

-> Add 'focus' fabric to your quilt in smaller quantities. This might include a center square in every block, the corners in a block on point, or the sashing of the quilt. When using a 'focus' fabric, the scrappy portion of the quilt will be more dominant, and the focus fabric exists within the design to unify the statement of the quilt. The guidelines for choosing colors for 'calm down fabric' will help you when you first start designing quilts with only 20%-40% focus fabric. In addition to the colors recommended above, red prints, solid red, and solid black all work well for center squares in your blocks and for cornerstones. As you get comfortable making quilts in this category, you may want to include complementary families of prints as your focus fabrics. The possibilities are endless, and you will develop your own artistic voice that is like no other as you gain experience.

-> When choosing fabric for sashing, I like to choose dark fabrics with a small print, or a medium print with a dense ground behind it. I typically cut my sashing in 2½" wide strips because I usually use 2½" squares in my blocks. If I don't have enough fabric to make sashing the way that I normally do, I will occasionally make my sashing 1½" wide, and in cases of extreme desperation, I will make it 1¼" wide. Skinny sashing has a completely different 'feel' in a finished quilt, and I encourage you to try using it in some of your designs. Because the blocks are physically closer together, skinny sashing unifies a quilt top more than normal sashing, which bisects your overall designs and strengthens the divisions between individual blocks. Conversely, if you want to strongly emphasize the blocks in your quilt, a wide, dark sashing (3" or 3½") will help your blocks 'float' like a picture in a mat within a frame. Also consider layering multiple 'frames' and sashing around individual blocks for more variety. This is a great way to de-emphasis ugly blocks.

-> Cornerstones should be made of a 'loud' fabric that stands out from both the blocks and from the sashing around them. Solid red, red prints, gold or cheddar prints, white on white, beige, black, and black prints all work exceptionally well as cornerstones. If you are playing with the cornerstone variations listed in the sidebar, any fabric with a small print will work, but the colors you use should have high contrast. (If the fabrics are too similar, you will lose the effect of the piecing, and would be better served to save yourself the time it takes to make the cornerstone units.) Adding cornerstones to a quilt with slightly messy blocks will help you force the fabric to make a neater quilt.

-> Backing choices are highly personal, but should relate to the front of the quilt in some way. 1930's reproduction quilts should have a plain white backing. I like to use plain black backing with art quilts, modern quilts, and some oriental quilts. I often use large prints for backings, although subtle, low contrast prints also work very well. Your long-arm quilter may grumble, but large scale stripes and border prints also look lovely. Your binding fabric should work very well with your quilt top, but should also visually unite the quilt top and the quilt backing. For binding, I like small, dense, low contrast prints.

ScrapStashtic Quilts

Design Troubleshooting

What do I do if my blocks are ugly?

1.) Try cutting your blocks into units within a larger block. For example, an ugly rail fence block can be cut and sewn into a block-sized half square triangle. If it's still ugly, cut and sew it again until it's a bowtie or a rectangle with a contrasting corner.

2.) Try turning your blocks on point and adding large 'calm down fabric' corners. Assemble the top with sashing or with sashing and cornerstones.

3.) Try framing your blocks with borders of varying widths. This idea could also play along with turning your blocks on point. The more layers of design you add to your oddball blocks, the prettier your awkward blocks will look.

4) Build new blocks from coordinated fabric. Cut apart the awkward blocks and use them in the same way you would use a 'calm down fabric.'

5.) Build another set of coordinated blocks and mix them in with the ugly blocks.

Keep in Mind:

If your blocks don't look good, chances are it is the colors/prints that are making your classic block look strange. Adding more fabric to your palate will help all of the colors get along, like the six degrees of Kevin Bacon. If you connect enough Hollywood Stars together, you'll eventually find somebody who has worked with Kevin Bacon. If you add enough different fabrics to your quilt's color palette, you will eventually have so many colors that the 'ugly ducklings' will blend in.

Design Troubleshooting

What do I do if I have redesigned my project and I have too many blocks?

1.) Don't be afraid to vote certain blocks off the island. If your quilt looks better without a particular block, or you have made one or two blocks too many, set aside the rejects and move on with your project. Check out the Fugly Quilt Recipe in the extra credit section; there may be a good home for your surplus blocks.

2.) If you have a LOT of extra blocks leftover after your re-design, set them aside until you have finished your current project. Then, pick them back up, and design a new (often smaller) quilt around the orphans. One time, I made 3 queen sized quilts and 1 craft sized quilt out of a collection of fabric that was supposed to produce a quilt for a double bed. All 4 quilts were completely different from each other, despite the fact that they all used the same color palate.

What if I don't have enough blocks?

If you find yourself running short of blocks, there are several things that you could do. If you are only missing one block, consider adding a center medallion or an autograph block with a meaningful message. If you are several blocks short of the number needed for the desired quilt size or pattern, you should consider designing a different layout. If you really have your heart set on one particular layout, you could add focus fabric in place of every other block, depending on the recipe. If the size of the quilt is the problem, you could add a very wide strip of sashing or several smaller borders around the quilt to increase its size. (If you use a wide border, I highly recommend using a different quilting design for the center of the quilt than for the borders. That wide, solid space can provide you with the perfect opportunity to highlight a particularly beautiful or unique quilting design. If you are having trouble visualizing this, there is a great example in the gallery of my website. The quilt is a mix of small panels, mixed 4-patches, and blank spaces embellished with machine quilting.)

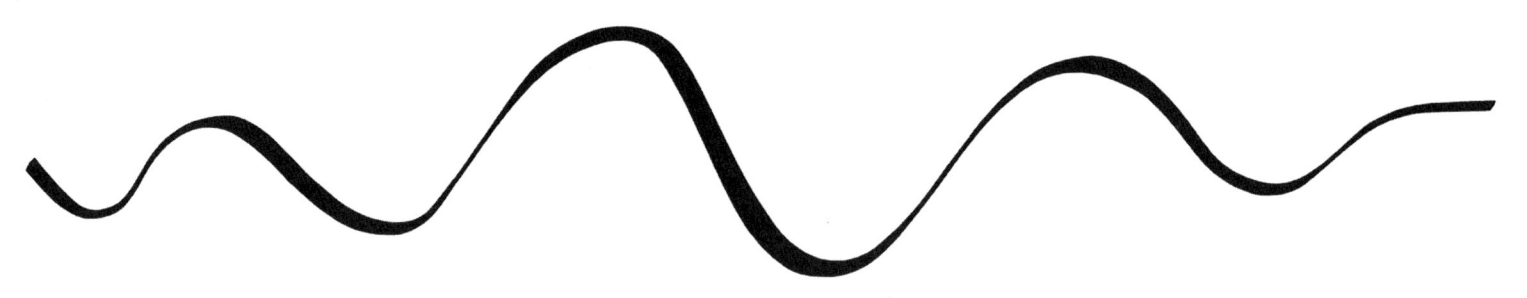

Scrap-Quilt Definitions

Everyone has a slightly different idea of what the language surrounding scrappy quilting means. Just to clarify, I've included some definitions as I use them in this book.

-> Make-Do-Scrappy: This is a completely random quilt, made only from fabric that is already in your house. These quilts are not necessarily wince-worthy, though. Some of my quilts that end up looking the most planned are Make-Do-Scrappy.

-> Planned Scrappy: Technically, this type of quilt is anything that is made with a planned outcome in mind. Quilts in this category include 'light and dark quilts' (also called 'sunshine and shadows' quilts), quilts that cluster around one or two contrasting color families, ombre quilts, or quilts that mesh scraps and Calm-Down Fabric in an all-over design.

-> Growing Quilts: This is a precursor to improvising quilts. As you grow a quilt, start at the center with a pieced medallion, then progressively work your way out with borders, pieced borders, rows of blocks, and sashing. Color palate can be pre-planned or can adapt as the needs of the quilt change.

-> Calm-Down Fabric: Yardage used to mellow the chaotic effects of scrappy quilting. Commonly used in vernacular phrases as 'calm – the – #### – down' fabric, calm-down fabric can account for up to 60% of a scrappy quilt.

-> Focus Fabric: Yardage used to consolidate the artistic statement of a quilt. Focus Fabric helps your eye move around a finished scrappy quilt. Multiple pieces of Focus Fabric can appear in the same quilt, and work nicely together when they are from the same fabric line or have highly contrasting colorways.

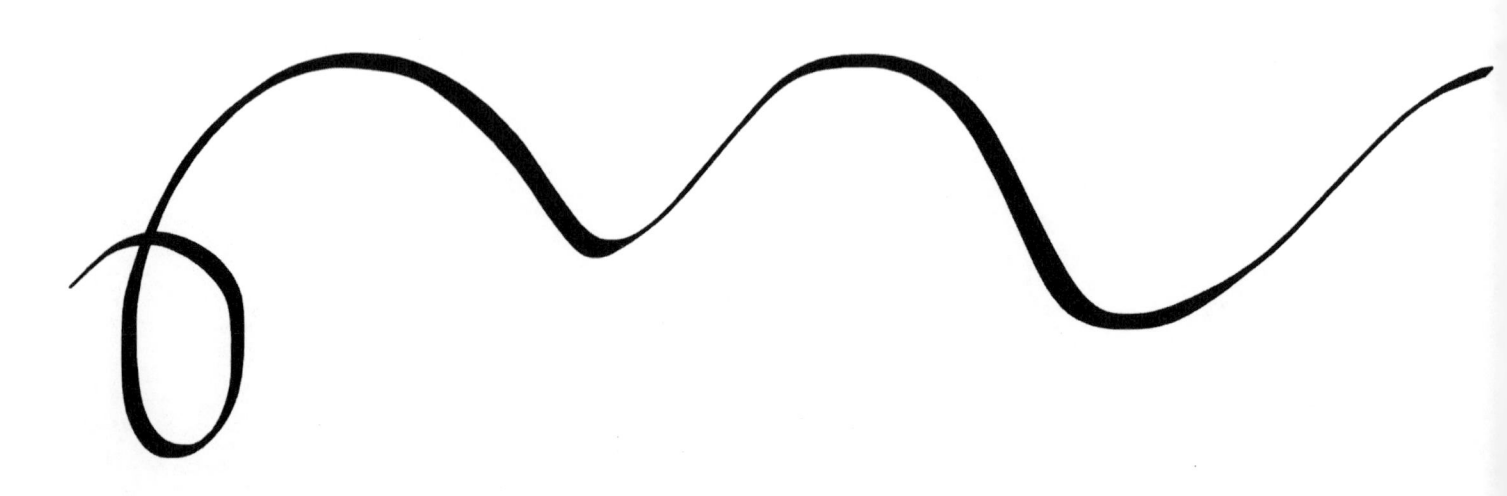

Nuts And Bolts

This section consists of a few random, technical pieces of information you may enjoy and find useful.

The ScrapStashtic system is a mutating system that I developed over the course of two years, and then spent another three years perfecting. It grew organically out of my quilting habits, and I built the structure of the system to support the way that I sew and the way that I interact with my fabric.

Because of the developmental and improvisational creation process, my system will 'play in the sandbox' with patterns and methods developed by other quilters. As your comfort with scrap quilting increases, I encourage you to stretch your creative boundaries, and see what other scrappy methods appeal to you.

The sizes that I chose for my precut fabrics were selected based on the sizes used in my non-scrap quilt patterns. Three quarters of the books on my sewing room shelf rely heavily on the sizes in the ScrapStashtic System. The benefit of using sizes that lend themselves to following other people's patterns is that you are able to adapt almost any pattern into a scrap quilt. Read that again. I can adapt almost any pattern to rely on my precut scraps, and so can you.

There are also many great rulers out there that provide easy stash-busting methods, which can further push your creative boundaries. Initially, I wanted to make do with one ruler for my cutting mat, and one ruler for my travel kit. Can you guess how that worked out? First my mom gave me a specialty ruler, then my mother-in-law gave me another... I inherited a portion of someone's stash, I borrowed a specialty ruler from a friend, I bought a stash from a non-quilting beneficiary... Since my 'one ruler' law was broken, I have been collecting specialty scrap rulers when they strike my fancy. Nine times out of ten, however, I reach for that same ruler that I started quilting with when my mother decided that I was finally old enough to touch a rotary blade. I'm actually on my third or fourth version of that same ruler (my cats like to scratch their faces on my rulers and knock them on the floor).

When I am cutting a traditional quilt, I flip my cutting mat upside down. Measuring with the ruler instead of the cutting mat gives you better precision with the rotary cutter. Using the reverse side of your mat forces you to rely on the ruler's measurements, only. This trick also has the added benefit of saving wear and tear on your cutting mat. (I destroy at least one mat every year through hard use, so this is an especially appealing habit to cultivate.)

When I am carving up scraps, I like to use the grid on the mat to measure my fabric and my cuts. When I am cutting up regularly shaped scraps (like a skinny ⅛ yard, a fat quarter, or the square scraps from a fat quarter) using the mat to measure gives me the fastest cutting speed possible. I cut from right to left, pinching the cut fabric out of the way with the rotary cutter still in my hand. Schnitzels get swept across the board and dumped into the stuffing bin on the floor. My left hand, alone, operates the ruler. (When I measure with the ruler instead of the matt, it usually takes both hands to straighten the ruler. I know it doesn't make sense, it's just one of my quirks.)

When I am fussy cutting irregular scraps into precuts, I also like to use the grid on the mat to measure. Having the full-sized grid allows me to use my eyes to try out a few different sets of 'real estate subdivision' before I start to cut. If I am having a hard time visualizing my strategy, I just start laying extra rulers on top of the irregular scrap to find the best/least wasteful plan.

Extra Credit
For the truly committed scrap quilter

Here are some project recipes you may or may not want to try. If you are truly committed to reducing your quilting waste to zero, forge on! I am proud of you and credit you with tons of brownie points.

Fugly Quilts

Fugly Quilts (or FREAKIN' UGLY quilts) are just what they sound like. They are overwhelmingly scrappy, and I generally make 1-2 of them every year. I save all of my leftover blocks, the extra units from my primary quilts, and the tails from my strip pieces. When my Fugly Quilt Storage unit fills up (not listed in the primary system because it is an extra credit project), it's time to make a Fugly Quilt. I randomly sew the blocks and leftovers into whole cloth, then design a quilt using the 'made' fabric against 'calm down fabric' or with blocks from a line of fabric. The results are always eye catching and command your attention. The Fugly Quilts have a strange beauty that you can't describe, you can't explain, and you can't escape. Even if you don't like the Fugly Quilt you just made, you HAVE to look at it.

> Believe it or not, the quilt on the cover is the 'fugly quilt' I made for my editor.

Monsters

My monsters are not a quilt pattern, but rather a stuffed animal recipe for using up the schnitzels in your stuffing bin. Every time I have made a set of monsters, my daughter and her friends have ransacked the collection before I send the rest of the toys to a local charity. (So, clearly, this pattern has been kid tested!)

Aside from the fact that the toys made from this recipe are cute, I find it appealing for several reasons. First and foremost, the bodies of the monsters are made from non-quilting fabric that finds its way to my house, but rarely gets used. (I have never purchased fabric to make monsters, and I will be surprised if I ever do.)

The second reason that I like them (aside from the fact that they empty my schnitzel bin) is that they are a quick and easy project. Most soft-sculpture patterns are adorable but very LABOR intensive. I've spent 40 hours on ONE stuffed animal. (Never again!) Even spending 3-4 hours on a stuffed animal that you are donating to charity gets a little tedious. The last time I made a batch of Monsters, I made 27 of them in less than ten hours. (Way less.)

ScrapStashtic Quilts

Directions:

Lay out two layers of fabric that are about 15" tall, and as long as a yard or two. With a rotary cutter, freehand cut curvy triangles. The base of each triangle should be about 6-10 inches long, and the tip of the triangle does not have to come to a perfect point. Cut as many as you like. I like batches of 8-12, although you may want to only do 2 the first time you try this recipe.

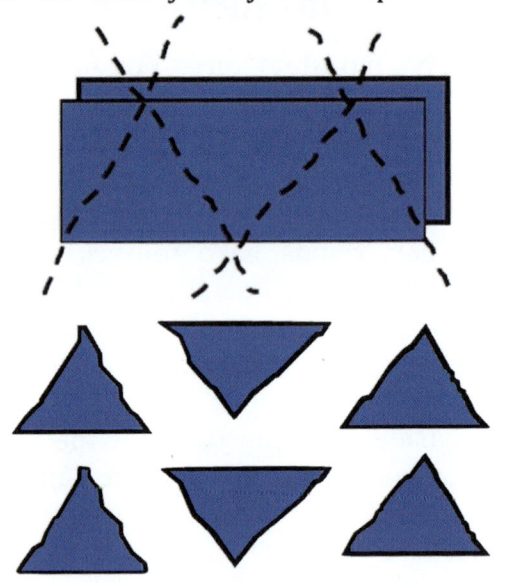

Sew the sides of the triangle together, then turn and stuff the animal. Sew the bottom closed by hand. Cut one eyeball from white felt or wool. (One eyeball is cute on a monster, two are creepy. Trust me, I've tried it.) Embroider a pupil in black, then use the black embroidery floss to sloppily stitch the eyeball to the monster. Stem stitch a mouth. You can use the pictures I've provided for inspiration, or you can check out cartoons, comic books, and coloring books to incorporate new facial expressions for your monsters.

Don't be afraid to make these lopsided, asymmetrical, or even square. Here are some of the monsters from my last batch:

How d'ya like them Apples?

This is a Schnitzel Bin busting project that I like to whip up when I need a quick, impersonal gift or set of gifts. I have gifted this project to teachers, colleagues, and casual friends. The finished project adds a beautiful design element to any room, but also serves as a great game to amuse visiting children. They can also double as Christmas tree ornaments. I like to put the finished apples in a wire basket from the dollar store, although I have also up-cycled traditional baskets.

60

Extra Credit

Using a red cotton print, cut out between 4 and 12 sloppy circles that are approximately 8" in diameter. If your circles are a little bit sloppy, your finished apples will turn out a bit more organic and folk-y looking. Using green double-knit gabardine (my favorite for this project because of how it looks and the fact that you don't need to hem it!) or green felt, cut out 1 or 2 free-hand leaf shapes for each apple. Separately, take a 4" - 7" piece of twine or jute and knot it into a loop. Make sure the knot is fairly large. (Note: The loop is optional. It is shown in the diagrams, but not in the pictures below.)

Returning to the red circles, make a large running stitch (by hand) half an inch from the edge of the circle. Draw the thread in to gather the circle halfway into a ball. (Make sure you are using a fairly strong thread so that it doesn't break. Button cord works very well for this.) Stuff the apple with your schnitzels, and place the knot of twine in the opening. Draw the thread the rest of the way through and finish cinching the apple closed.

Tack the gathers together, reinforce the loop, and sew the leaf onto the top of the apple at the stem. Repeat until each gift basket is full.

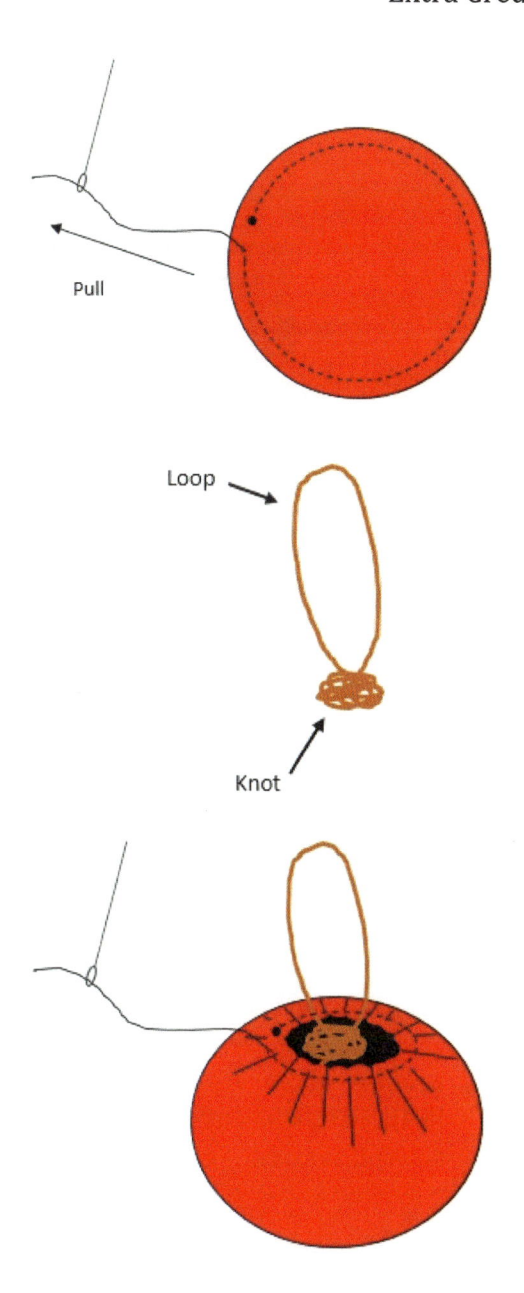

61

About the Author

Janellea Macbeth is a creative individual who 'arts' her way through life and spends capacious amounts of time playing with fabric. An avid hand, machine, and long-arm quilter, Jan has been sewing for 31 years and quilting for 25 years. She has introduced many friends to the delights of cutting fabric into little pieces in order to sew it back into large pieces of fabric, and hosts QuiltingFriends.weebly.com from her cell phone. She is joined in her sewing room exploits by her cats, who just want to help with EVERYTHING, and a dog who very respectfully naps through every sewing session.

Stay in Touch with the Author

I really hope you enjoyed my book! Quilting is such an important part of my life, and I really enjoy making new quilting friends. I would love for you to contact me and keep in touch, in one of many ways:

First, please visit my website, www.janelleamacbeth.website/. There, you will find information about books I've written, a picture gallery, and my blog. Most importantly, however, you will also find the opportunity to sign up for my newsletter. This is a spam-free newsletter, and I only email a few times a month. Topics will vary from new ideas that might interest you, the occasional special promotion, and cool stuff I am giving away, such as signed copies of my book or free, top-notch quilting goodies!!!!

Next, I'd really like to get your opinions of the book. I would REALLY appreciate it if you would leave a frank and candid review on Amazon! Reader reviews are the lifeblood of any author's career. For me, as an author, getting reviews (especially on Amazon) means I can submit my book for advertising, which means I can actually sell a few copies from time to time. Every review means a lot to me!

I'd also like to get to know you and keep in touch. You can find me on Facebook at www.facebook.com/amored.flaneur?fref=nf. Don't worry; I don't overuse my Facebook the way many people do. Rather, it serves as a great way to share ideas, videos, and inspiration with other quilters and artistic crafters from all over.

Additionally, I would love to hear about your ideas, opinions, projects you are working on, books you are reading, or any quilt wisdom you would like to share. I especially love to celebrate 'Ah-ha!' moments and finished projects. Quilt pictures are welcome! Feel free to post to my Facebook, or send me an email at amored.flaneur@gmail.com.

Printed in Great Britain
by Amazon.co.uk, Ltd.,
Marston Gate.